# DOVES AND DOVECOTES

# DOVES AND DOVECOTES

Peter and Jean Hansell

## Millstream Books

*This book is dedicated to all those*
*who have in any way*
*recorded, maintained or restored dovecotes*

First published 1988

Millstream Books
7 Orange Grove
Bath BA1 1LP

This book has been set in Baskerville type direct from the authors'
Amstrad PCW8512 discs by Saxon Printing Ltd, Derby
Printed in Great Britain by The Amadeus Press, Huddersfield

© Peter and Jean Hansell 1988

ISBN 0948975113

# Preface

Dozens of dovecotes are still dotted about the country today, many of them hidden away and hitherto unnoticed. They are survivors of the many thousands that were built from the time of the Normans onwards to house the pigeons which were bred for the larder. They are of all ages and range from ancient, rugged, utilitarian structures to the elegant architectural fancies of the 18th century. Their present fascination lies not only in this wide diversity of style but also in the fact that no two dovecotes are identical in every detail.

Descriptions of dovecotes by authors past and present have largely been confined to local regions. The only broad picture ever to have been attempted was published more than fifty years ago, since which time the scene has changed. It is hoped that this book will fill the gap to some extent. Its aim has been to highlight the remarkable variety of surviving dovecotes in various parts of the country. In achieving this end, information and illustrations have been garnered from countless sources and it has been possible to include a comprehensive bibliography. But nothing can approach any sort of completeness without that element of personal study, field work and literary research which we have pursued over several years. From all this emerges the fact that there seems never to have been any systematic approach to the appreciation of dovecotes and their inhabitants, nor any attempt to categorize the types, styles and fancies. This, then, constitutes the main framework of our endeavour.

Hence, apart from passing reference to France, Scotland and Ireland we are chiefly concerned with the inclusion of representative examples, both past and present, within our chosen classification. The object here has neither been to provide any sort of gazetteer, nor to be restricted to a particular area, but rather to select buildings of merit and differing architectural styles, from the earliest to the more recent, including those which have captured the fancy of some of our greatest architects.

There can be little doubt that dovecotes are an attractive and irreplaceable part of our heritage, but their numbers have been decimated over recent centuries and even today they are falling down; more surprisingly, a few have been under threat of demolition quite recently. Current concern for conservation, together with the statutory listing of buildings of architectural and historical importance, now expanded to include vernacular architecture, should ensure preservation of worthwhile examples, but in practice some still seem to slip through the net. In addition to the ravages of neglect, decay and destruction there is increasing pressure at the present time to convert larger dovecotes into habitable dwellings — an opportunity boldly proclaimed in the property advertisements and which seems to gain assent; but is this the best solution?

The principal subject of these pages concerns dovecotes, but it would not be complete without mention of the pigeons who once occupied them, whose descendants in their thousands now inhabit most major cities. Their grey bobbing forms must be familiar to every town dweller, but their remarkable story is more elusive. Sadly they have fallen from favour and are regarded generally as a nuisance and at best are merely tolerated. Their special links with man and their great service to him in the past are largely unrecognised or forgotten and justify a reminder here.

This account does not purport to be exhaustive and it is hoped that dovecotes will repay chronicling for some time to come, before others join the toll of those lost for ever. If this book does anything to foster an awareness of the need for continuing conservation, its aim will have been achieved.

*Let no man who writes a book presume to say when it will have finished. When he imagines that he is drawing near to his journey's end, alps rise upon alps and he continually finds something to add and something to correct.* (Edward Gibbon)

P.H. and J.H.
Bath 1988.

# Contents

*CHAPTER I*

# The Bird

Any study of dovecotes must include consideration of the birds for which they were originally built, whose descendants now throng squares and piazzas all over the world. Nowadays, the busy grey pigeons on the pavements and sidewalks are regarded by many as a pest and civic nuisance, but their history and unusual character are largely unknown.

No other bird has had such close links with man, nor been useful to him in so many ways. It has served him as symbol, sacrifice, source of food and, not least, as messenger. It has also played a minor role as bait and decoy in the ancient sport of falconry and was massacred by the dozen in the pigeon-shooting matches of the 19th century. Today, the gentler pursuits of pigeon fancying and racing both have a large following in many parts of the world. In such activities the strong bond of affection that often exists between owner and birds is not widely appreciated.

**Origins**

The complete story of this remarkable bird has been much obscured by the age-long confusion between the terms 'pigeon' and 'dove' both of which are still used loosely and interchangeably today. It is not readily perceived that both the Old Testament dove of Noah and the New Testament dove of the Holy Spirit are the ancestors of today's multitudes of urban pigeons. Nor does there seem to be an obvious resemblance between the white dove of peace and the pigeon in a pie, but all these birds are directly descended from the Blue Rock Pigeon which is found in the wild everywhere in the world except at the polar caps. The bird makes its natural home in the rocky ledges and niches of maritime and inland cliffs, but it has an inborn affinity with man and a tendency to nest in and around his dwellings to the extent that in the first place it probably domesticated itself and man may have done no more than meet its advances half way. The feral birds of the towns originated largely from domesticated pigeons which had escaped from dovecotes and nowadays they appear in every sizeable city.

The general appearance of the pigeon is well described by its Latin name, *Columba livia*, which translates as the dove or diver bird of leaden or blue-grey colour. Its rather drab look is relieved by two black bars on the wings, best seen when they are folded, and a white rump, but its brightest feature is an iridescent greenish-purple patch on the neck and upper

9

Victorian collage from Charles Knight's *Pictorial Museum of Animated Nature*, 1896

breast, which is most pronounced in adult males. In the days when the pigeon was in high favour this feature was highlighted in a lengthy anonymous English 18th century poem of rhyming couplets, devoted entirely to praising doves and giving advice on running dovecotes:

> *Sometimes you'd think about their neck was roll'd*
> *A glittering brede of saphyr mixt with gold*
> *Sometimes the Carbuncle's more vivid light*
> *Dazzles the Eye and hurts the feeble Sight.*

Natural variations in colour and pattern among wild, domesticated and city birds are often seen and add interest to the breed. The pure white mutation which occurs infrequently is very beautiful and must have excited a certain degree of wonder among the ancients to whom it became the white dove of symbolism, religion and art.

Although the familiar plump, pink-breasted, white-collared wood pigeon, the stock dove and several other foreign varieties are members of the same genus, *Columba*, they are quite distinct from the Blue Rock Pigeon and do not interbreed with it. They also have totally different characteristics, in particular a marked reluctance to become domesticated, a habit of roosting in trees rather than on rocky cliffs and an absence of the gregarious instinct. The collared turtle dove belongs to another order altogether and resembles the pigeon only in name; it has recently settled in the British Isles having spread westwards from the Middle East during this century. It was, however, well-known in the remote past when its migratory habits and its characteristic wheezing cry were remarked. The Song of Solomon includes both doves (pigeons) and turtle doves quite separately.

**Etymology**

Several names for the pigeon have entered the language and have been retained in one form or another. The Anglo-Saxon 'culver', also 'culvour' and 'culfre', were in use in the third century and have survived chiefly in south-western parts of the country where the usage persists as 'Culverhill', 'Culverfield' and 'Culverwell'. Generically it has also been adopted as a surname as seen in the current London telephone directory which lists three dozen 'Culvers' and 'Culverhouses'. The Latin *Columba* is no longer in common use but the flower 'Columbine' and a patron saint of Scotland, St Columba, are both named after it. 'Columbarium' meaning a dovecote was widely used and appears in many early records and documents. It survives today in Wales as 'colomendy' and in Cornwall as 'clummier'. The word 'pigeon' derives from the Latin *pipio*, meaning a young cheeping bird. It was probably introduced here at the time of the Conquest and has become closely woven into the language as in 'pigeon-holed', 'pigeon-breasted', 'pigeon-toed' and 'it's not my pigeon'.

'Dove' first appeared in Chaucer's time as 'duva' or 'douve', and is of Norse origin like the word 'squab' for the young bird, which comes from the Scandinavian *skvabb*, meaning anything soft and thick. It has given us 'dovetailed', 'dove grey' and 'lovey dovey' and from it comes 'dovecote' or 'dovehouse' and also the colloquial 'duffus' in East Anglia, 'ducket' in the north and 'doocot' in Scotland.

The very earliest meaning of *kolumbis* in Greek, *columba* in Latin and 'dove' in Anglo-Saxon was in each case the diver bird. This puzzling derivation may have described the male bird's characteristic diving movements of the head during the bowing display of courtship.

## Characteristics

GALLICE Coulon, Colombe.
GERMAN. Tub/ Taube/ Zame taube.

Columba Anglica uel Ruffica, Palumbus cicur.
GALLICE Pigeon paté.
GERMAN. Zame fchlagtub/ Welfche tub/ Gehofflete tub.

The pigeon has several biological quirks which must have marked it out from the very beginning. It has been described as a 'wonderfully fruitful bird' and in favourable conditions a pair of birds raise their brood of two as frequently as ten times a year. They are not only assiduous and protective parents, but the secretion by both male and female of 'pigeon's milk' to feed their young strangely resembles a mammalian function and is unique in the avian world. The pigeon's way of drinking 'uphill' with its beak and nostrils submerged and without tipping back the head to invoke the aid of gravity like other birds is another singular feature. Its roosting posture, in which the head drops forward with the beak resting on the breast instead of being tucked under the wing is also unusual. A strange anatomical variation is the absence of a gall bladder; a deficiency with which Shakespeare was familiar when he wrote 'I am pigeon-livered and lack gall to make oppression bitter'. Most remarkable of all is the pigeon's superbly developed homing instinct. This gift, which is combined in flight with great reserves of endurance, must have seemed magical to the ancients and even in this scientific age is not fully understood.

More important than such physical characteristics is the pigeon's unusual and attractive character which has endeared it to man since time immemorial, although nowadays it has fallen from grace and has come to be regarded as the least romantic of birds. It combines conjugal affection with utter fidelity to its mate and this devotion makes the birds fret when parted, as is quoted in the Book of Isaiah: 'We mourn sore like doves'. Present-day racing-pigeon breeders recognize separation as being the mainspring which drives the bird back to its nest. A recent account of the overt mourning of a pigeon, on discovering the dead body of its mate, illustrates such behaviour in extremity. This bird persistently nudged and

12

pecked the corpse as if trying to revive it and alternately covered it with outstretched wings.

Pigeons, particularly those feral birds who live in the cities, are demonstrably resourceful. They scurry about the squares and pavements searching for morsels of food and roost in rows on building ledges above. In London the birds have even penetrated the underground railway system and a few may be seen actually riding on trains. All this is considered by some to be a nuisance and is a cause of concern to civic authorities. Notices in the city which prohibit the feeding of birds are largely ignored and do nothing to curb such attention in Trafalgar Square.

Public notice at a London
Underground railway station

## Symbolism

In the world of symbolism the pigeon or dove has filled several different roles. It was venerated in many ancient civilizations to which it represented the virtues of love, gentleness, fidelity, purity and innocence. Later, it became endowed with the quality of mercy as is embodied in the device of a dove which surmounts the rod of equity carried by the English monarch during the Coronation ceremony. But the very earliest association was much more primitive and stemmed from the bird's sexual prowess and

13

Deities and Doves in classical antiquity

14

great fecundity which linked it with the fertility or mother goddesses of the Middle East and Eastern Mediterranean. Clay images of doves resting on the heads and hands of such deities, dating from 3000BC, have been excavated in Crete and Iraq and similar terracotta votive offerings have been found in shrines of the goddess Ishtar or Astarte, whose ancient worship was prevalent in Assyria. She was a descendant of the early fertility goddesses and was later taken over, together with her doves, by the Greeks as Aphrodite. In Roman times she became known as Venus, who was often depicted in a chariot drawn by a pair of doves. The birds thronged the temples of these goddesses, where they lived alongside the sacred prostitutes.

In ancient Greece, they played an important role in the oracular ritual, probably a cunning exploitation of their homing ability. Perched on the sacred oak trees at the Temple of Zeus in Dodona, their murmurings and coos were interpreted by the priests and priestesses as messages from the god. All these temple birds were regarded as sacred and it was forbidden to kill them for other than sacrificial purposes. Such circumstances provided an ideal milieu for domestication, however unintentional.

The bird was also revered in the Hindu religion. It is recorded that in the India of early times the pigeon and owl were symbolic messengers of the King of the Dead. Shiva, the third god of the Hindu Trinity, is said to have found some of his human followers so exasperating that he turned them into pigeons and they have haunted his shrines and temples ever since, hoping for release.

In the Muslim religion, the birds also held a special place. It was claimed that the prophet Mohammed received divine messages through the medium of a dove sitting on his shoulder, but it had in fact been trained to peck grains of wheat from his ear. Large flocks hovered around the mosques, particularly at Mecca, where nesting places were provided and pilgrims purchased grain with which to feed them.

It seems likely that the pigeon was the only domestic bird known to the Hebrews of old and certainly no bird is mentioned more often in the Old Testament. The familiar role that it played in the catastrophe of the Flood inspired its symbolic meanings of good news and deliverance; also peace which was connected with the olive branch even before the Flood. These attributions are still universally understood today.

The dove as a symbol of the Holy Spirit plays a significant role in Christianity. It is a recurring simile in the New Testament and is frequently depicted in Christian legend and art. A dove was the special emblem of Pope Gregory the Great and the magnificent statue in the Vatican shows one perched on his shoulder.

In this country the bird is linked with a number of saints, the best-known being Scotland's St Columba, but also the lesser-known St Kenelm. He was a son of the King of Mercia and was murdered as a child by his sister.

Legend holds that the tragedy was miraculously notified to Rome by a dove which alighted on the altar of St Peter's bearing a message in its beak.

Even until quite recently the bird was used in parts of Europe as a living religious symbol during some traditional celebrations of the Christian calendar, when tame white pigeons were released during the solemnities. In Venice during the Palm Sunday Procession of the Guilds in the Piazza of St Mark, the Comb and Lantern Makers' Guild carried a cage of birds which were released in the Doge's presence. Descendants of these Venetian birds were protected and fed in the Piazza at public expense until the 1920s.

Today, on a more secular occasion, the opening ceremonies of the Olympic and Commonwealth Games are marked by the release of a flight of white doves simultaneously with a fanfare of trumpets and raising of flags. In this context the custom may have been intended to symbolize peace because when the original Olympic Games were inaugurated by the Greeks, all warfare was banned during the month in which they were held. Alternatively they may have been liberated as messengers to carry news of the event to distant parts. A similar gesture is depicted in an early Egyptian bas-relief showing the lavish coronation procession of a king in which the birds can be seen being released from their cages by the priests.


## Sacrifice

The sacrificial offering of a pigeon was a common practice in the distant past. In Egypt it is recorded that King Rameses III offered more than 57,000 birds to the god Ammon at Thebes towards the end of 1100BC. In ancient Greece, Ovid refers to the cages of sacrificial doves which were on sale outside the temples, particularly those of Aphrodite. In the Old Testament the dove was the only bird singled out for this purpose, but it was especially a poor man's offering, a substitute for the more costly kid or lamb. In the New Testament two pigeons were the chosen sacrifice on the very special occasion when Mary brought the child Jesus to be presented at the Temple. Much later he drove out the money-changers and the dove-sellers.


## Messengers in Peace

The pigeon's ability to return to its nest from considerable distances must have been recognized in the early days of its domestication. It was evidently known to Noah. Breeding and training of the birds as messengers started in the Middle East aeons ago and much later spread to Europe. In England, pigeons were not widely used for the purpose until the 19th century although it is known that they were introduced from the East much earlier. A century previously, the writer John Moore gives the impression that the birds were still an exciting novelty: 'And such is the admirable Cunning or Sagacity of this Bird that tho' you carry 'em Hoodwinkt twenty or thirty miles, nay, I have known 'em to be carried three score or a hundred, and there turned loose, they will immediately hasten to the place where they were bred'.

Apart from the story of the Flood in Genesis and the parallel Greek and Babylonian accounts, the earliest written reference to such use of the birds is the *Ode to the Carrier Pigeon* written by a Greek poet in 532BC. In later Roman times, Ovid, writing at the beginning of the Christian era, described a pigeon, dyed purple for easy identification, being sent home by a youth with news of his success at the Olympic Games. Half a century or so earlier, Varro wrote about the Roman ladies who were in the habit of taking tame pigeons to the amphitheatre where they 'let them loose from their bosoms' during the spectacle to fly home ahead. Was this merely a diversion or were they taking back some domestic message? In England, nearly two millenia later, before the days of telegraphy, away-supporters of early football matches used the same means to carry home news of the score as the game progressed.

The earliest large-scale network of communication using pigeons is believed to have been established in Assyria and Persia by Cyrus the Great in the 5th century BC. Much later, in the 12th century, Baghdad and all the main towns of Syria and Egypt were linked in this way and the birds continued to be used right up until the introduction of the telegraph. In several ancient maritime civilizations pigeons were released from homeward bound ships nearing port to carry advance news of the cargoes on board. In 14th century Turkey, pigeon towers 40 miles apart straddled the country and were manned by sentinels who transferred messages onward from one bird to another; fallibility was safeguarded by sending a duplicate message two hours after each bird had been released.

A 5th century Chinese reference to the use of pigeons for carrying personal correspondence describes the method of attaching the message to the bird's leg. Centuries later, western missionaries in Shanghai observed the large number of carrier pigeons that were kept in the city and noted the devoted care given to them by their keepers. These birds were used commercially to carry trading news between towns as well as from incoming junks. The custom probably continued unbroken until the 19th century, at which time numbers of pigeon keepers were in business to transmit news, particularly between bankers and money changers, as well as to send results to students of the prestigious literary examinations of the day. The curious present-day custom of attaching 'pigeon whistles' to the birds has been followed in Peking since AD1100 and was originally believed to ensure a safe passage for the messengers. These devices,

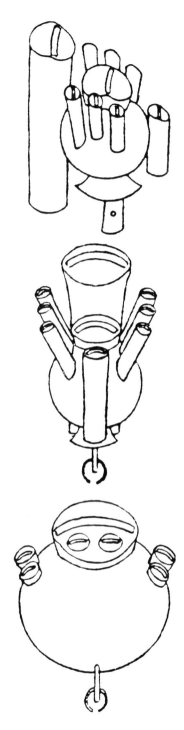

Chinese Pigeon Whistles
(actual size)

17

consisting of small bamboo or gourd pipes, resembling tiny Pan or organ
pipes, are secured either to the bird's leg or, more commonly, in an upright
position to the two middle tail feathers near the rump. The whistles make
musical noises in flight which are described by the Chinese as heavenly
music or the sound of the spirits of their ancestors. Early western observers
drew the conclusion that the object of their use was to scare away hawks
and other predators, but it has recently emerged that the custom was
intended purely for aesthetic pleasure. In other parts of the East as in
India and Bali, little bells are used in the same way. In England, in the high
days of falconry, the legs of newly-trained hawks were sometimes fitted
with two tiny silver bells, generally one semitone apart, chiefly for the
purpose of recovering birds lost in dense cover.

Peaceful uses of the birds as messengers seem to have arrived relatively
late in this country although trained carrier pigeons were brought to
Europe from Persia in the 16th century and long before that, returning
Crusaders must have been familiar with the custom. It was not until the
19th century, when a pigeon post became established in Europe, that they
were used extensively. The birds were quicker than the mail coaches and
provided a valuable adjunct to other means of communication. When
Baron Reuter started his well-known organization for collecting and
transmitting news, he employed pigeons, not only in addition to telegraphy, but also to fill missing gaps in the railway networks, particularly
between Berlin and Paris. Day-to-day news, especially in the money
markets, depended on speedy and accurate information in which messenger pigeons played a major role. In England, a pigeon post was

18

established by *The Times* newspaper between Paris and Boulogne and stockbrokers set up pigeon lofts at Dover and Folkestone. A message from the Bourse in Paris arrived much quicker by pigeon than by the mail and large fortunes were sometimes made on the Stock Exchange by this strategy. At the end of the century, pigeons were being used regularly by the *Daily Graphic* to convey news of events at home, such as the Boat Race and the Derby; the time taken from Epsom to the office in London being recorded as 20 to 25 minutes. At sea, early salvage operations also used pigeons to keep in touch with base.

## Messengers in War

The pigeons' record as messengers in time of war is a moving and little-known epic. Scattered references describe the many feats of bravery and endurance which have been carried out by these valiant little birds.

In the far distant past, news travelled between armies by riders on horseback or runners on foot, both of whom were slower and more vulnerable than the birds. Julius Caesar is said to have made use of pigeons during the conquest of Gaul, as did Hannibal while crossing the Alps. Pliny mentions them as carrying despatches during sieges and cites the Battle of Modena in 53BC. When Acre was besieged during the Crusades, centuries later, Richard I's adversary, Saladin, kept in touch with the garrison by means of carrier pigeons. The English discovered the ruse when a crossbowman shot down one of the birds. Venetian annals reveal that, after the fall of Constantinople in 1204 during the Fourth Crusade, the Doge sent the good news home by a carrier bird which had to fly 700 miles to Venice. It may seem incredible, but is not impossible; modern racing pigeons have been known to cover distances of 1000 miles and more.

When specially bred and trained carrier pigeons were first introduced to Europe from the Middle East in the 16th century, their military potential was recognised from the start. In Holland they were used by the Prince of Orange in 1572 to help maintain the morale of the citizens of Haarlem who were under siege by the Spaniards, and the birds were similarly used by the beleaguered Venetians during the siege of their city in 1849. But the best known achievement took place during the siege of Paris in 1870-71 towards the end of the Franco-Prussian War, when carrier pigeons were flown out with refugees in balloons and were established in lofts outside the battle zone. In *The Old Wives' Tale*, Arnold Bennett gives a graphic description of the nocturnal departure from the Gard du Nord of one of these balloons together with its two passengers and six caged white pigeons. Apparently, of the 65 balloons that left Paris during the siege, two, of which this was one, were lost and never heard of again. In England, the General Post Office arranged for correspondence to be sent to the

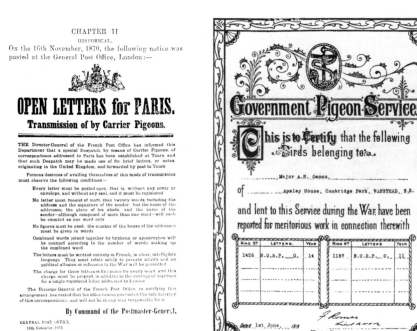

*(left)* Pigeon post from London in the Franco-Prussian War
*(right)* A pigeon's War Service record

besieged citizens of the city using the pigeon post for the last half of the journey on the other side of the Channel. Messages in the form of miniature photographic images were carried from London to Tours by ordinary mail and thence to the pigeon lofts, from which the birds carried them onwards to Paris. In spite of the Germans' efforts to intercept them by deploying hawks, many pigeons succeeded in reaching their destination and the ensuing publicity helped to popularise the sport of pigeon racing and was responsible for the establishment of military pigeon stations in Europe at the end of the century.

At the outbreak of the First World War, the British authorities, fearing that some of the large number of racing pigeons in private lofts might be used for espionage, banned the transit of all birds and at the same time ordered owners to clip their wings. Many were spared this confinement, however, and eventually breeders gave an estimated 100,000 birds to the war effort. Unlike the other European allies, who had established military lofts, the British depended entirely on voluntary cooperation.

Pigeons were much used in mine-sweeping trawlers during the early stages of the war before wireless had been fitted. In a successful U-boat attack, an SOS message carried by a bird often enabled the crew to be saved from their sinking ship. In military action on the front lines in Europe the pigeons were kept in mobile lofts behind the trenches and often had to fly through gun barrage and poison gas to deliver their messages to base. At home, fixed lofts were maintained at all important aerodromes and a line of them was established along the east coast from Newcastle-upon-Tyne to

20

Hastings for use in the event of invasion. In addition, all the crews of tanks, seaplanes and submarines were trained to handle the homing pigeons which they carried.

The bird's role in the Intelligence Service was important in maintaining contact with sympathizers and resistance movements in enemy-occupied territory and during such missions it has been estimated that only ten per cent returned. Batches of pigeons, each in its own container with a little parachute attached were taken by plane across the Channel. The ingenious contraptions which were used to deliver them were splendidly basic, but seem to have operated well. Each unit comprised a large parachute from which several containers were suspended. When jettisoned from the plane, a clockwork mechanism operated to release each one singly as the whole contrivance floated down to earth. Inside each container was also a bag of corn, a note requesting intelligence, propaganda messages and the promise of a reward. The risks to the bird were considerable; if not found, they died of starvation and if discovered by the enemy their only hope of survival was to be released with a counter-espionage message as did sometimes happen. The Germans threatened the death penalty to anyone involved in such subversion.

The improved use of telecommunication in the Second World War reduced the need for pigeons to some extent. Nevertheless, thousands of birds were given to the National Pigeon Service by British breeders at the outbreak of war. They were used not only in the European theatre but as far afield as India and Burma. The American Services also had their own pigeon units in many countries. As in the previous war, the birds were employed in the British Intelligence Service and often accompanied our agents when dropped by parachute. Invaluable details were relayed back about the German V1 and V2 rocket sites on the other side of the Channel. They were also carried routinely on bomber planes and were again particularly useful in sea rescue emergencies. At the time of Dunkirk, birds in east and south coast lofts were enlisted as part of an anti-invasion scheme, but fortunately were not needed.

## Memorials

Many of the pigeons' feats during both World Wars led to human lives being saved and were recognized by appropriate awards. But for every deed identified there must have been dozens which went unsung. In the animal world, the Dickin Medal is regarded as the equivalent of the VC and was named after its founder, Mrs Dickin, who also started the People's Dispensary for Sick Animals. One of its early recipients in the First World War was a cock bird known as 'Red Cock' who delivered a message from the mortally wounded captain of a torpedoed trawler which led to the crew being rescued. The captain was awarded a posthumous VC and the bird was nicknamed 'Captain Crisp VC' in his memory. In the Second World War, a hen bird was released with a message from a Beaufort bomber which had ditched and broken up in the sea more than a hundred miles off the Scottish coast. Although covered with oil and soaked in salt water, she managed to reach base enabling the crew to be saved.

Many notable incidents also took place on the battlefield. On the Western Front in the First World War, a French pigeon which nearly died on its flight through smoke and poison gas, delivered its vital message to base and was eventually awarded both the Croix de Guerre and the Légion d'honneur; today a memorial to it stands in Verdun. In Brussels a more imposing edifice commemorates the 21,000 Belgian pigeons who lost their lives in the Great War. In this country, there is no monument on such a scale, but at the PDSA Animal Cemetery an individual headstone marks the grave of 'Mary of Exeter' who played her part in the last war. This hen bird flew many missions, was often wounded and at one time bore 22 stitches in her tiny body.

### Source of Food

Among the pigeon's several roles none has been more important than its use as a source of food. It has indirectly left monuments of a very different kind in the form of capacious dovecotes in which the pigeons lived and multiplied. Although no longer used for their original purpose, those which still stand today are reminders of a widespread custom that was of major importance in the domestic economy for centuries. The bird's considerable contribution to the kitchen covers such a wide front that it merits a separate account.

*I am a friend of the pigeons but I also enjoy them on my table. Also don't forget that gastronomy apart, they are the image of the Holy Ghost.*
(Roger Peyrefitte, Paris, 20th century)

# CHAPTER II

# Culinary, Medicinal and Sporting uses of the Bird

> *No man need ever have an ill-provisioned house if there be but attached to it a dovecote, a warren and a fishpond wherein meat may be found as readily at hand as if it were stored in a larder. Certainly a vast pigeon and rabbit pie is a most useful standing dish in a country house for members of the family and for chance droppers-in, and then if properly managed there will always remain somewhat to sell over and above what is consumed at home.*

So wrote Olivier de Serres in his book on agriculture and husbandry published in 1600. There was nothing new in his advice at that time. The living larder that he described had already become a well-established custom in medieval England and pigeons from the dovecotes were regularly on the menu both here and in several other parts of the world.

## As Food

In Mediterranean countries the pigeon and the goose were indigenous at a very early time; the domestic hen was introduced later from the Orient.

Although the evidence is sketchy, pigeons appear to have been a favourite table fowl in ancient Egypt. They are depicted on decorative reliefs and wall paintings and sometimes appear on tombs where the birds are seen being carried either dead or alive as food offerings to the deceased. In addition to such pictorial records, pigeons were mentioned in the diet as early as 3000BC and actual pigeon bones have been found in the remains of a funerary meal at an excavated tomb of the same period. In later times under Roman rule the pigeon house tax levied by Augustus indicates the size and importance of the pigeon economy which in those days supplied manure as well as food on a large scale. On a more homely note, an extract from a papyrus written by the master of a household in the 2nd century gives an amusing glimpse of domestic life and shows that the birds were regarded as worthwhile gifts: '...the pigeons and small fowl which I am not used to eat...send to the teacher of my daughter that he may be diligent with her...'

In Rome, pigeons are mentioned in that most ancient of European

cookery books written by the rich Roman gourmet Apicius in the time of the Emperor Tiberius during the first century. It includes several recipes for sweet and sour spiced sauces to accompany roast or boiled pigeon squabs and recommends that the birds should be boned before being cooked. Almost two millenia later, Mrs Beeton also advises boning the birds in some of her recipes.

In England, numerous culinary references to the pigeon in early medieval times show that it was not only a delicacy, but a regular item of diet. A 14th century cookery book gives a recipe for stewed pigeons thus: 'Take peions and stop them with garlec ypylled and gode herbes ihewe', while another work mentions a different method altogether: 'Mijnce ye rostid peions'. At that time the birds were often roasted on spits, carefully sewn up at each end to prevent the much-prized gravy from escaping. The young unfledged birds — the squabs, squeakers or peesers — were particularly suitable for roasting in this way. They become tender and succulent after only twenty minutes cooking, unlike older birds which need a much longer and slower method. Even today, recipes in French cookery books characteristically specify the use of young birds.

Surviving domestic records, the keeping of which was customary in most households of any size from the 13th century onwards, also give useful information about diet and confirm that even at everyday meals, fowls and pigeons were generally part of the menu. An entry in the daybook of Dame Alice de Breyne in 1413 records the daily provisions for the household as 'one quarter of bacon, one capon, two chickens and twenty pigeons'. Extracts from the Bishop of Hereford's domestic accounts which were compiled by his chaplain during one year at the end of the 13th century reveal that 'the tables on flesh days were never spread without a due proportion of birds and poultry of some kind, even if it were only a dish of larks and pigeons'. Apart from the daily routine, there were also occasions for great feasts. At a banquet held by the Earl of Warwick in 1470, it is recorded that 4,000 pigeons were served together with vast quantities of meat, fowl, game and fish of all varieties. This orgy of protein was served with sharp, spiced sauces and accompanied by soups and sweet tarts; no vegetables appeared on the menu in those days. It is puzzling to find so little reference to pigeons' eggs being consumed, although like those of hens, they would have been useful on Fast days. Possibly, the squabs were too highly valued to be aborted in this way; a rare 18th century allusion seems to confirm that the eggs were not customarily eaten, 'and though Hennes are more fruitful in laying of eggs, yet pigeons are more profitable by often bringing forth young'.

To judge from the size of early monastic dovecotes and surviving documentary evidence, pigeons made a considerable contribution to the diet in religious households in spite of several restrictions. In the early days of their foundation, several orders abstained from eating the meat of

24

quadrupeds, but the biped fowls and pigeons were sometimes allowed. The strictness of the rule varied; in some cases it was general, but in others it applied only to the many Fast days in the calendar. However, it was invariable during Lent, both inside the monasteries and among practising Christians outside. Special dietary allowances were made at all times for visitors, the sick and elderly, and periodically for those monks undergoing their seasonal bleeding therapy at the infirmary. Over the centuries these exemptions opened the way for a certain laxity so that the saying 'gluttony was the darling vice of the monasteries' may well have become justified in late medieval times. All in all, the dovecote pigeons must have been in steady, if not increasing, demand right up until the Dissolution.

From the time of the Conquest onwards, in addition to owning dovecotes, landowners, both religious and secular, enjoyed the privileges of emparking for deer, building rabbit warrens and keeping fishponds, salmon-coops and swanneries. All these sources of protein supplied the larder throughout the year and were valuable supplements during the winter months, when the so-called great meats comprising beef, veal, mutton and lamb were in short supply. In early times, meat constituted an essential part of the diet and the English had gained a reputation for being great flesh eaters and for cooking meat to perfection. Accordingly, the customary slaughter in November of most farm stock, apart from those kept for breeding and working, due to lack of winter fodder, was felt to be a great deprivation. In Henry VII's time fresh meat was seldom eaten, except during the short interval between midsummer and Michaelmas, even by the gentlemen attendant on a great earl. Preservation of the meat of slaughtered animals in brine or by dry salting or smoking was effective, but proved monotonous and the fresh meat from the dovecotes with occasional poultry, game and rabbits provided a welcome change. But of them all, the pigeons probably played the major role.

The pigeons' steady cycle of breeding ensured a regular and dependable supply of meat at all times. Each pair of birds produces two chicks eight to ten times a year for about seven years and during this time the parents fatten the squabs with their own regurgitated 'pigeon's milk'. The young birds were generally culled at the age of four weeks when still covered with down and before the pin feathers had developed. At this stage the flesh is tender, juicy and fat, without any trace of the toughness brought about by the exercise of flying.

Although every kind of wild bird also featured on the medieval menu, much time and energy was expended in catching them for the pot. Fowlers using traps, nets, decoys and limed branches pursued them relentlessly. In addition, hunting and, later, shooting provided a sporting supplement to the larder. Compared with these sources, however, pigeons and barnyard fowl were not only more conveniently at hand, but they had the added advantage of being available to eat at all seasons and without the need to be

*Columba hirsutis pedibus*
*A rough footed Dove.*

*Columba Numidica seu Cypria*
*a Barbary Pigeon*

*Columba tremula laticauda*
*A broad tailed Shaker*

hung like many game birds. Hence the wide popularity of the old recipe known as spatchcocked pigeon. The term derives from 'despatch' meaning to kill quickly and 'cocked' which was used when cock birds were culled from the dovecote. In the kitchen the bird was sliced down the middle, flattened out like a kipper and grilled on either side for ten minutes. It was a quick and useful dish for the chance guest and was on the menu in taverns and post-houses where pigeons were generally kept in the yard. An 18th century diary entry illustrates its usefulness:

> *On Monday we took a coach and four and went with a very honest clergyman to his little vicarage house in the Isle of Thanet where we went into the Dove House, killed a dozen pigeons, pluckt them, spitted 'em, roasted 'em and eat them ourselves.*

Even after the introduction of winter feeding for animal stock by agrarian pioneers, such as Jethro Tull and Charles 'Turnip' Townshend at the end of the 17th century, pigeons continued to be eaten although not on such a large scale as before. In the prosperous days of the 17th and 18th centuries, great variety in the menu was customary in substantial and moderately-sized households and numbers of dishes were needed to ring the changes. Pigeons appeared in many guises and the numerous recipes that have come down to us, ranging from humble pigeon dumplings to the grand 'Patty of Pidgeons Royal' illustrate their versatility and continuing popularity. Simple methods included stewing, braising, jugging and cooking in a 'hole', like toad-in-the-hole, or in the popular pigeon pie, known in Scotland as 'doo tairt', which was a favourite Sunday dinner. In addition there were several weird recipes, for example, 'Pigeon Transmogrified' meaning to alter greatly with grotesque or humorous effect, in which the cooked bird was stuffed into a large hollow cucumber or small marrow with its head and legs protruding at each end and a bunch of barberries in its mouth. 'Pulpatoon of Pigeons' was a lavish dish with a forcemeat crust containing kidneys, mushrooms, chestnuts, pigeons and artichokes. A delicious, but extravagant, method was to remove the breast from the bird and fry it in butter. This recipe was derived originally from the French as *pigeon au soleil* and later modified to become English pigeon fritters. Another popular method from France was to combine the small, sharp-tasting vineyard grapes with stewed pigeons; such ingredients would have been readily at hand as dovecotes are often situated in the vicinity of vineyards. In England, the combination of pigeon and asparagus is mentioned in the 18th century, but is not heard of nowadays, unlike the traditional duck with peas which is still very popular. Preservation of various foodstuffs was practised early on and recipes for potting and pickling of sparrows, squabs and larks appeared from the 17th century onwards. The birds were either baked in wine and butter for a

26

long time and then sealed in pots, or boiled repeatedly in a pickle of wine and vinegar, herbs and spices, until the bones had been dissolved.

## Commercial Rearing

*Columba gutterosa*
*A Cropper dove.*

Pigeon pie, described in the 16th century as a 'food fit for kings', travelled across the Atlantic to become a national dish in America. The custom of pigeon rearing was no doubt familiar to the early settlers and references show that pigeons were bred for the table at an early stage. However, it was not until the setting up of commercial squab production at the beginning of this century that pigeon meat ceased to be a delicacy and became widely popular. Subsequently it was said that every family expected to eat squab at least once a week. Some of the early pigeon farms were very large indeed and housed more than 10,000 birds while a few were said to accommodate 30,000. The popularity of the birds was due not only to their delectability and availability, but also to the fact that game birds and some wildfowl were protected by the Government's rigid game laws following their earlier decimation.

*Columba tabellaria*
*A Carrier-Pigeon.*

During the First World War the American people were urged by the State to breed their own squabs, the merits of the case being succinctly promoted as follows:

> *Grow squabs in your backyard. Take little room, grow quickly, are easy to raise. The pair of pigeons Noah took into the Ark could nest, hatch and raise a pair of squabs in the forty days the rain lasted. The eggs of pigeons hatch in seventeen days. The squabs are ready to eat in three to four weeks. No other domestic bird or animal can make its meat product in so short a time and repeat seven or eight times a year. Nothing easier to raise. Nothing better to eat.*

*Columba domestica major*
*a Runt.*

In this country, commercial pigeon farming has been practised only sporadically and on a small scale. There was some slight enthusiasm for the business between the wars and in 1971 squabs for consumption were being bred in Kent . A more recent resurgence of interest was mentioned in the quality press of 1985 under the title 'Chic Choice for Christmas'. The report described Norfolk-bred squabs as being plump, tender, juicy and delicate; but they were expensive to buy! At about the same time a different journalistic approach provided advice on economical catering to those on hard times and recommended pigeons and rabbits as being cheap sources of protein. However, the few birds on sale in the supermarkets and on the butchers' counters today are adult wood pigeons which are very delicious if cooked slowly and for a long time, but not comparable with the tender young dovecote birds. Many current cookery books still contain methods for cooking pigeons, but in one of the glossy versions published by a large chain-store the recipe for squab pie contains no pigeon at all.

**Medicinal Uses**

The pigeon not only featured regularly in the diet of the past, but eating it was believed to prevent certain diseases. In the 17th century it was held that pigeon flesh protected against the plague and several other unspecified illnesses: 'Those who make it their constant and ordinary food are seldom seized by the pestilential diseases'. Other miscellaneous conditions against which it was claimed to have prophylactic properties included short-sightedness, palsies and tremblings. Eating squabs during convalescence was particularly recommended to build up the patient's strength and was still being advocated in the 18th century as a general remedy: 'They are nourishing, somewhat binding, strengthening and provoke urine: they are looked upon to be good for cleaning the Reins (kidneys) and to expel the Gross Matters that stick there'.

The pigeon itself provided important ingredients in many of the superstitious and sometimes gruesome remedies contained in the early antidotaries and pharmacopoeias. A particularly bizarre procedure which was still popular in the 17th century consisted in the application to the patient's head or soles of the feet of a live pigeon cut in half which, it was said, 'clapt hot upon the head mitigates fierce humours and discusses melancholy sadness'. Several other conditions were claimed to respond to this therapy which may have owed its efficacy as much to the psychological shock as to its unpleasantness. In his diary, Pepys describes the classic instance in 1663 when Charles II's Queen 'was so ill as to be shaved and pigeons put to her feet'. A quite different, but also macabre remedy involved the application of the anus of a pigeon to a snake-bite wound as a first aid measure. Was the object of this strange manoeuvre based on the neutralising effect of bird lime?

Several concoctions for both external and internal use incorporated various parts of the bird and its by-products. As far back as Roman times, Pliny mentioned the instillation of pigeon's blood as a cure for bloodshot eyes. The remedy may have been founded on that ancient philosophy of like curing like and many centuries later it was still being used. An even more disagreeable notion of making the bird's sifted dried dung into a poultice or salve for external application was still being advocated in the 18th century. Using it as a base, several combinations have been described as, for example, mixed with watercress for baldness and gout, or with barley flour and vinegar for tumours, or with salt and oil for 'defluxions of the knees'. Potions based on the prepared dung were even prescribed for internal ingestion, in particular as a means of 'expelling urine and

28

breaking the stone'. A brief mention of its inclusion in clysters or enemas illustrates the bizarre directions in which such empiricism could lead.

## Folklore

Part of the myth and magic of ancient times were the many homely superstitions that prevailed. Doves and dovecotes being so closely knit with domestic life, it was natural that several sayings and old wives' tales should be woven around them. Some carried gloomy predictions such as the saying that he who pulled down his dovecote would bury his wife within a year, while another held that the gift of one would bring bad luck to the recipient. It was also believed that the possession of a dovecote prevented the course of true love running smoothly. In the West Country, a strange white pigeon hovering around the house was supposed to herald a death in the family, while in mining districts a pigeon flying round the pithead was a bad omen. On a more cheerful note the arrival of a strange bird in the dovecote was believed to bring good luck.

A curious old hunting custom in France entailed smearing the hunts-man's bullets with pigeon's blood in the belief that they would more readily find their target.

The feathers and down of pigeons, like other farmyard fowl, were customarily used to fill pillows and feather beds, a fact that was evidently familiar to Shakespeare and described by him, 'as soft as dove's down and white as it'. There was a common superstition that those who slept on pigeon feathers would live to be a ripe old age. Of course the charm could not be guaranteed and one particular failure is recorded by an early Scottish author: 'But she died and on a bed of pigeon feathers too, to the dismay of all the wise women of Cromarty'.

## Fertilizer and Gunpowder

It is written in the Second Book of Kings that at the time of the great famine during the siege of Samaria, 'an ass's head was sold for four score pieces of silver, and the fourth part of a cab of dove's dung for five pieces of silver'. A cab was a Hebrew measure roughly equivalent to two quarts and the quotation illustrates the high value placed on this dovecote product in very early times. In the Middle East, particularly in Meso-potamia, eating pigeon flesh was forbidden and dovecotes were built primarily to provide manure for melons and they continued to be used for this purpose for many centuries. In France, Italy and Spain the droppings were much valued, largely for fertilizing the vineyards and occasionally for hemp fields. In this country several early writers on husbandry considered the bird's dung to be much more potent than other farmyard manure; it was said that one load was worth ten loads of other sorts. It was applied to the hop fields and also more generally to other crops, both at planting time and as a later dressing: 'No manure makes the Corn more strongly rise, or the Grass please with brighter Green the eyes'.

In England, towards the end of the 16th century, the dung from the dovecotes was also used as an important source of saltpetre for the manufacture of gunpowder. The secret of this process had been brought over from Germany in 1560 and divulged by a German for a payment of £300. At that time there were no known natural resources of saltpetre and collection of manure from stables, farmyards and even domestic households was authorized by Charles I in 1627. Initially this intrusion was much resented and subsequently dovecotes became the chief sources of supply. It has even been suggested that some were specially built on this account. Further legislation forbade owners to pave dovecote floors with stone or brick, only good mellow earth being allowed. However, they were entitled to compensation for any eggs or birds lost during collection of droppings, the duration of which was restricted to two hours each day and only at convenient times. Records show that the production of gunpowder was almost a monopoly in Surrey where there were about 18 mills at Chilworth, but there was some production elsewhere, as in Hertfordshire. The industry was relatively shortlived, however, and ended with the discovery and exploitation of naturally occurring saltpetre in South America and the East Indies at the end of the 18th century.

The sport of 'Owling'
(Henry Alken, 1821)

30

The dung of fowls and pigeons was also employed by tanners to produce a slight degree of putrefaction in animal skins that were to be used for making soft leather. This process effectively removed the hairs and subsequently the contents of the pit were used as liquid manure.

## Sport

The ancient sport of falconry was enjoyed in this country even before the Norman Conquest. It has been called the 'Sport of Kings' and the Bayeux tapestry shows Harold carrying a hawk on his gloved hand. The pursuit remained popular with the court and aristocracy until the advent of the shotgun at the end of the 17th century, from which time onwards a diminishing number of enthusiasts carried on the tradition. It still has a considerable following among the privileged few in the Middle East where pigeons are still used as bait. During the sport's heyday in England, a few varieties of hawk were trained to fly at pigeons in the field, in particular the tiny but beautiful merlin, which was traditionally flown by ladies and beginners. Even in those early days, however, the practice of using 'bagged quarry' from the dovecotes, rather than birds in the wild state, was regarded by some as being a trifle unsporting.

During the training of hawks, dovecote pigeons were sometimes flown as an alternative to the more customary feathered lures. Even more cold-blooded was the tethering of a live pigeon to a perch on the ground to attract a recalcitrant hawk, hence the derivation of the phrase 'stool-pigeon'. This method was practised on a large scale in Holland to decoy falcons and hawks on their migrations. At North Brabant, families of falcon-catchers gathered annually for this purpose, after which the birds were sold at a great fair and auction.

The pastime of 'owling' which enjoyed a brief vogue in the 18th century, exploited the tendency of birds such as pigeons to mob owls in daylight. A trained owl on a string was made to perch on top of a pole. Limed crossbars lower down entangled the mobbing birds as they alighted so that they were easily caught. A similar custom is still prevalent in the Himalayan region and is painfully reminiscent of the current Mediterranean practice of netting migratory birds which have been cruelly trapped on limed branches.

The introduction of firearms in the 17th century made possible the wholesale shooting of every type of bird and the blue rock pigeon was no exception. This bird was always regarded as good sport because of its speed and evasive agility in flight. Its natural home on the rocky coast of north-west Scotland provided an interesting variation in which guns were aimed from a boat below the cliffs at birds flushed from their caves. Enthusiastic sportsmen have described the excitement of this pursuit

Pigeon-shooting Match,
Hurlingham Club, London 1869

which is still carried on today in a few places: 'The rolling of the boat, the twisting flight of the pigeons and the distracting noise of the breakers, combine to try severely the best of shots'.

Pigeon-shooting matches in which the birds were released in one way or another became popular at the end of the 18th century. Substantial bets were often involved. Two of the best-known early meeting places were at Ealing and in fields bordering the south bank of the Thames at Battersea. At first, participants covered the hapless birds with their headgear before releasing them so that they came to be known as 'Old Hats' following the introduction of mechanical traps. Hurlingham Club was founded in 1869 expressly for pigeon shooting and quickly became the most fashionable venue in London during the summer months. Honorary members included the Prince of Wales (afterwards King Edward VII), and teams drawn from the Houses of Lords and Commons regularly competed against each other. Rules were formulated, handicaps established and the pigeons' welfare protected by the London Gun Club; it was claimed that the birds were treated as carefully as racehorses. Nevertheless, the sport was not without its antagonists as one critic records, '...where delicate ladies and highborn gentleman will spend their hours in critically watching pigeons mangled for wanton sport and for lack of something better to do'. Mounting opposition led to the sport being banned at Hurlingham in 1905 and although the pigeon-shooting members objected, a final lawsuit in the courts upheld the decision. In other parts of the country, however, rural matches continued covertly well into this century. In Sussex, pigeons from the Birling Manor dovecote were used for matches which took place beside East Dean church. In some districts, Boxing Day was traditionally celebrated with a pigeon-shooting match.

This sport depended upon a steady supply of dovecote birds, often six to ten dozen being required for each match. It is said that Sussex dovecotes charged one shilling for each bird, while in London considerably higher prices were paid, even as much as half a crown per bird. At Hurlingham, match-shooters were required to pay for the birds used on each occasion. It is not surprising, therefore, that there was a good deal of pilfering from dovecotes. The naturalist, Charles Waterton, writing in 1837, bemoaned the extent of the problem and the methods used by a 'plundering set of land vagabonds' who robbed the dovecotes, sometimes down to their last remaining birds. During these nocturnal exercises the birds were flushed from their nests by rattling the entrance door and were then trapped as they emerged from the dovecote by nets secured over the exits. Ten years ago there were still remains of iron security grilles at Ravenfield in Yorkshire, and the double metal dovecote doors at Purfleet, Essex, described by Donald Smith in 1931, prompted him to comment 'the whole reflects seriously upon the character of the neighbourhood and likewise upon the value of the contents of the dove house'.

Clay-pigeon shooting, in which saucer-shaped targets are catapulted into the air simulating the flight of birds, developed partly to fill the need of enthusiasts after live pigeon shooting had been banned, but was also intended for practice when pheasants and other game were out of season. The earliest targets consisted of hollow glass balls decorated with feathers, but in 1880 a quarry made of pitch and river silt had been devised and a mechanical trap to catapult them was developed at the same time. The sport soon became popular in its own right and went from strength to strength until today, under the aegis of the Clay Pigeon Shooting Association, it attracts a considerable following. Its popularity is no doubt enhanced by the absence of a closed season or any ban on Sunday meetings.

**4637. Barrett, C. J.,** [*Bloom, J. E.*]. Sept. 28. 1883.

*Trap-shooting.*—Relates to aërial or flying targets and traps for shooting the same.

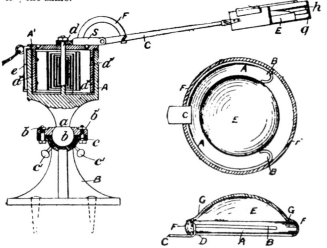

**4341. Pike, J. F.,** and **Pike, C. W.**
March 7. 1900.

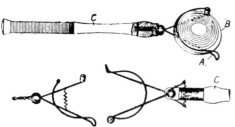

*Trap-shooting.*—Relates to apparatus for use in throwing " inanimate birds " for shooting practice.

**16,311. Edwards, E.,** [*Mitchell, H. S.*]. July 22. 1902.

*Trap-shooting.*—Relates to a hand trap for throwing clay pigeons or targets.

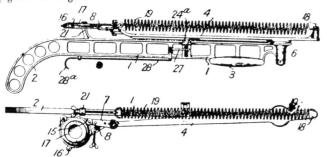

**10,628. Tranter, W.,** and **Dixon, C.**
July 26. 1884

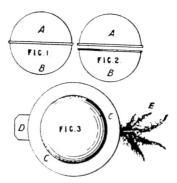

*Trap-shooting.*—The targets are made from thin sheet metal, and are filled with powdered charcoal, chopped feathers, &c

**6956. Mott, J. L.** April 4. 1895.

*Trap-shooting.*—The trap consists of a box A let into the ground, having a platform B and a hood C pivoted at 3 and provided with openings 6, for allowing light to enter the box, facing the direction in which it is desired the pigeon shall fly when released.

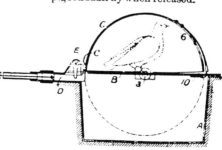

**7015. Macomber, L. H.** June 9. 1885.

*Trap-shooting.* — Relates to trap-shooting targets of semicircular or truncated cone shape, and of non-breakable material, which are thrown into the air with a spinning motion.

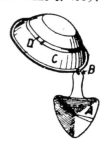

Patent descriptions relating to live and target trap-shooting

**3451. Kitson, J.,** and **Bulmer, J.**
Feb. 25. 1891.

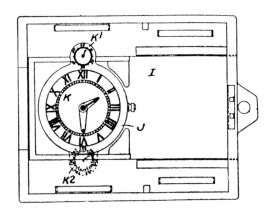

**14,067. Barker, F.,** and **Barker, C.**
June 25. 1896.

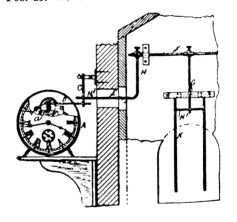

Patent timing devices for pigeon racing

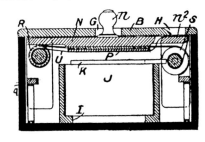

*Races, timing.*—The apparatus is intended principally for recording the departure or arrival of homing pigeons, but may be used for other purposes.

## Racing and Fancy Pigeons

The present-day pastime of pigeon racing has its roots in the ancient custom of using the birds as messengers, but the evolution of the modern racing pigeon in the West took place in the latter half of the 19th century, partly in Britain and the United States of America, but mainly in Belgium where it has been the national sport for more than a century. Today's racing pigeon fancier is generally a combination of owner, breeder, trainer and punter. The buying and selling of the pick of these highly bred birds is carried out on an international scale; a present-day champion recently fetched the phenomenal price of £42,000. Races are controlled by local clubs who supervise timing of the birds with specially designed tamper-proof clocks. Large pantechnicons with a capacity for several hundred birds, as well as sleeping accommodation for driver and custodian, collect and ferry the pigeons around the country and release them at appointed starting places. It is a far cry from the early days when they were taken by boat to Southampton or in horse-drawn coaches or even, until quite recently, in the guard's van of trains. At Marylebone

Oriental Frill
(from Fulton's *Book of Pigeons*, 1895)

Station in London there was a so-called 'Columbadrome' in which racing pigeons relaxed before being carried at special fares to their destination at Great Yarmouth.

Some racing pigeons are capable of flying at amazing speeds over great distances, sometimes achieving altitudes of 6,000 feet, and returning home with almost unfailing navigation. Such feats result from the bird's innate homing instinct which derives from its compelling need to hurry back to its mate in the nest. In addition, many experts maintain that the bond of affection between owner and bird which develops so readily in pigeons and which is encouraged in the loft from an early age, also spurs them on. The result of such early imprinting is illustrated by a recent anecdote in which a bird returning home at the end of a race tapped with its beak at the window of the kitchen in which the owner was having coffee, before returning to its loft. Sad to relate, many birds fail to complete the race and are lost. Some survive, however, and join the ranks of their cousins in the cities where they quickly settle down and adapt to the new life. Others are found, sometimes injured, but it is lamentable that few owners sustain any further interest in these losers, even when reported.

Runt
(from Fulton's *Book of Pigeons*, 1895)

The many exotic varieties of fancy pigeon which exist today have all been bred from one single species, the Blue Rock Pigeon *(Columba livia)*. This took place early on in many different parts of the world, chiefly in the Middle East and around the Mediterranean basin, but also in India, North Africa and the Orient. In the mid-19th century, Charles Darwin, who was himself a keen pigeon fancier and a member of two London pigeon clubs, demonstrated the common origin of the various breeds by meticulous investigation and estimated at that time that there were more than 150 separately named varieties which bred true, but nowadays there are many more. Included among this remarkable selection are the familiar White Fantails, the acrobatic Tumblers and Rollers, the grotesque puffed-up Pouters, the pretty Oriental Frills and the long-feathered, fluffy Jacobins. In addition to these fascinating and often very beautiful breeds there are

37

two important utilitarian groups, namely, the Persian Wattled pigeons from which the Carriers and Racing Homers were developed and the large Italian Runts, which were bred for size in ancient times and came to be known as the Roman Banquet pigeon. On the Continent, this culinary variety has been extensively bred for the table, giving rise to the well-known Carneaux and Mondaine strains which are said to have been introduced to some English dovecotes by the Benedictines. At Allington Castle there are still several red Carneaux birds nesting in the walls; they are thought to be descended from those which occupied dovecotes there in the 16th century.

Despite years of exploitation, persecution and indifference, there can be little doubt that much affection for our pigeons remains. Nowadays the emphasis of interest has changed and the enthusiasm for keeping racing and fancy pigeons still flourishes, while the city birds continue to give pleasure to young and old alike.

CHAPTER III

# Early Domestication and
# Dovecotes The World Over

Domestication of the pigeon, which broadly means to house and breed in captivity, was probably first attempted thousands of years ago. It was a far step from merely taming the bird and compared with other domestic creatures, more tricky. The great ornithologist, the Comte de Buffon, gave a neat summary in the 18th century of the particular vagaries of the dovecote pigeon.

> *It was easy to domesticate the heavy and inactive birds, such as the common hen, the turkey and the peacock; but to tame those which are nimble and shoot on rapid wings, required attention and art. A low hut, rudely constructed on a confined spot is sufficient for lodging and raising our poultry: to induce the Pigeons to settle we must erect a lofty building, well-covered without and fitted up with numerous cells. They really are not domestics like dogs and horses: or prisoners like fowls: they are rather voluntary captives, transient guests who continue to reside in the dwellings assigned them only because they like it and are pleased with the situation which affords them abundance of food, and all the conveniences and comforts of life.*

## Ancient Custom in the Middle East

In the remote days of pre-history, the pigeon probably nested in man's cave dwellings and in neolithic times moved with him into his first crude buildings. The bird is by nature very adaptable and has always been ready to find a congenial substitute for its usual rocky haunts in the various structures of civilization. All that it requires for its nesting place is some protection from the elements, so that any ledge, cleft, niche or opening of adequate size serves the purpose. When man's protection and encouragement was added in early times, eventual domestication became inevitable. The exact spot where this started is not known, but it is believed to have been associated with the cultivation of cereals and domestication of other animals in the alluvial plains around the Tigris and Euphrates from 8000BC onwards. In Egypt there are records of the custom and mention of the bird on a menu in 3000BC. From this part of the world the agricultural way of life spread across Europe and eventually into Britain. It is impossible to say whether the pigeon nest-holes recently discovered during excavations of neolithic stone dwellings at Skara Brae in the Orkneys owe anything to this influence.

Dovecotes consisting of square or diamond-shaped pots crudely made of clay and stuck together haphazardly are thought to have been built at a very early date in southern Palestine where pigeons are common in the gorges and wadis of the south. Modifications of similar structures persist in Egypt at the present time. Elsewhere in the Mediterranean, clay pots are still employed for the purpose, either within a dovecote or hung upon the outside walls of houses. A different form of dovecote in Egypt was described by Diodorus in 44BC. It was built of mud and had a conical reed-thatched roof in which holes allowed the birds to come and go. A primitive dovecote of this sort appears in the well-known Roman mosaic at Palestrina near Rome, which vividly depicts contemporary scenes on the banks of the Nile.

## In the Classical World

Although there are many allusions to the pigeon in Greek literature, the earliest descriptions of domestication and rearing birds for the table were given by Roman writers. They borrowed the Greek terms *peristerion* and *peristerotrophion* and used them in addition to their own word, *columbarium*, which suggests that the custom must have existed earlier in Greece. The writer Varro, who compiled a great library in the time of Julius Caesar, wrote extensively on agriculture and husbandry. A section of his work *De Rerum Rustica* is devoted to domestic pigeons and to the type of building in which they were housed. His description is so telling that it is worth quoting.

> *The* peristerion *is built in the shape of a large* testudo *with a vaulted roof. It has a narrow entrance and windows latticed in the Carthaginian fashion, or wider than these are, and finished in a double lattice so that the whole place may be well lit and no snake or other noxious animal may be able to get in.*

He adds that there were many pigeon cotes in Rome, Florence and in the countryside and that a single one often contained 5,000 birds. The Latin *testudo*, meaning a tortoise, was also the name for an arched roof and describes what must have been a domed building of roughly circular shape. Other writers of the time refer to dovecotes as monster beehives, a descriptive term still used today. Varro does not specify the building materials used, but does describe the interior walls and exterior window surrounds as being coated with smooth marble-dust cement. In addition to these detached buildings, pigeons were also kept in turrets on villa roof-tops in the towns or housed in the gable-ends of farmhouses.

As their empire expanded, the Romans took the custom of breeding pigeons into Gaul and later into England. It has been suggested recently that traces of Roman *columbaria* might be found in the vicinity of Romano-British villas and in some cases the archaeological evidence is suggestive. No superstructure remains, but the foundations of several square, rectangular and octagonal buildings adjacent to stables, granaries and barns have been excavated, although none with a circular base-plan as might have been expected. At that time domestic and farm buildings were customarily timber-built and were perforce square and rectangular in shape. Although no separate dovecotes of the Roman era have survived, niches that have been identified as pigeon-holes are still to be seen in the ruins of the Roman colony at Caerwent in Wales.

## Persian Dovecotes

In parts of the Middle East where pigeon rearing had its ancient origins, the custom has persisted over the centuries until quite recently. In some districts of Persia, dovecotes of exceptional size and elegance have survived from the 17th century when they were built by the monarch of the day. A traveller to Isfahan a century or so after their construction, the Frenchman Jean Baptiste Tavernier, reported that he had seen a total of 3,000 dovecotes, some of which were 70 feet high, housing more than 10,000 birds. They were not eaten by the Shia Muslims; the initial function and sole importance of the pigeon house was to provide manure for fertilizing melon plants. At that time the privilege of building a dovecote was much sought after in Persia, but was restricted on religious grounds to Muslims, as Tavernier says, 'some of the vulgar sort will turn Mohammedan to get that liberty'. A later visitor, the Englishman James Morier, when on a mission to the King of Persia, also drew attention to the dovecotes, which he described as being splendidly painted and ornamented and much grander than the dwellings of the populace. Many of these buildings have survived and can still be seen today, although most of them have been deserted by the birds and are falling into disrepair now that artificial fertilizers have taken over. Some are massive, drum-shaped buildings which stand conspicuously in the open fields of melons and sunflowers like rows of medieval forts or Martello towers. Others are smaller and built as slender conical towers which house far fewer birds and are generally situated in or near villages. Summit openings for the pigeons in both types consist of one or more perforated turrets which give an attractive chequer-board effect in the distance.

41

Persian Pigeon Tower

## Pigeons in Egypt

In Egypt, pigeon rearing has been an essential activity for centuries, not only to provide meat, but also manure. The fertility of the Nile valley has always depended greatly upon this source partly because, in times past, the dung of other farm animals was used as fuel. Dovecotes tended to be clustered in certain regions and C.S.Sonnini, a traveller from France in the 18th century, drew attention to those he had seen at Alguan in Lower Egypt: 'I never saw so many dovecotes together in one place in my life'. He

42

was a naturalist and collaborated with the French ornithologist, the Comte de Buffon, which may explain his interest.

Today, pigeon breeding is carried out on a small scale in many villages where bottomless clay pots are built into the parapets of mud houses, beneath which branches are fixed as perches. Others consist of clay pitchers stuck roughly together in columns, while there are also large, detached pigeon houses of several types which dominate the landscape. Some are very spectacular indeed and even qualify for entry in the current Baedeker's Guide to Egypt. Distinctive designs are to be found according to locality. Near Cairo, slender white conical towers, 50 feet high, each one dotted with small apertures, are grouped together in small or large numbers. At the nearby Fayoum oasis, large edifices constructed of mud and pottery comprise tier upon tier of units with many circular holes, the whole building roughly tapering upwards. Another pattern in Lower Egypt consists of a massive cylindrical or square base surmounted by numbers of little cupolas arranged in circles around a central dome. This is said to be a design influenced by features of the local mosques.

Further south in Upper Egypt in the region of Thebes (Karnak), Luxor and the great oasis of Kharga the construction is completely different. These pigeon houses are in the form of solid, square-based tapering towers, truncated at the top, which resemble the ancient pylons flanking the temple portals in the vicinity. In the upper parts of the buildings, large numbers of leafless branches are embedded in the outer walls to provide perches for the birds. Palm-leaf mats are arranged beneath them to catch the droppings. Nowadays, chemical fertilizers are fast outmoding the use of pigeon manure in Egypt, but the birds are still very popular as a delicacy and the national dish of grilled pigeon is still traditionally eaten at the end of the annual spring celebration, the Great Bairam.

Dovecotes of Alguan, Egypt
(from an 18th century engraving)

43

*(top)* Present-day dovecote at Fayoum Oasis, Egypt
*(bottom)* Cluster of tower dovecotes near Cairo

44

Pigeon-fancying in India

## The Far and Middle East

In far eastern countries, pigeons have been valued for centuries, but with more emphasis on their use as messengers and as fancy varieties. In India, the birds have always been sacred to the Hindus and are much protected by them. They nest in all sorts of public buildings and are not molested or killed. It is not known when they were first domesticated, but it is recorded that in the 16th century one of the Mogul Emperors kept a number of breeds including one variety for carrying messages. Merchants from abroad brought back new foreign birds to add to his collection and he received others from the King of Iran. The custom of breeding fancy pigeons was very popular in both India and Iran and many of today's species can be traced back to these sources. There are few recorded details of housing for the pigeons in these parts, but in India a very unusual method of keeping the birds underground was still being used in some villages quite recently. Bottle-necked 'wells' are sunk eight feet deep in the ground, the interior being lined with nesting places for the birds; possibly an ingenious method of protecting them from the scorching sun, which is also still used in Algeria and parts of the Middle East. Even stranger ways of housing pigeons have been exploited in Turkey. The extraordinary

La Colombier de Vanjoyeux,
a well-restored French dovecote

see page 65

volcanic landscape of Cappadocia contains churches, dwellings and dovecotes, hollowed out in the rocky cliff faces and in the fantastic massed tufa monoliths which occur in some parts.

## Continent of Europe

In the west, there is little doubt that pigeon breeding for food, fertilizer or fancy spread around the Mediterranean basin and thence across Europe. Even today there are dovecotes still standing in Greece, Italy, Spain, Germany, Holland and, of course, France, where in the 17th century there were estimated to be 42,000 dovecotes, which is almost twice as many as there were in England at the same time. Exceptions to this general distribution seem to be the Scandinavian countries and Switzerland, where few if any are to be found, probably due to the lack of large tracts of arable land.

46

*CHAPTER IV*

# Interiors and Management

The inside of a large dovecote can be a most impressive sight. The walls of the dimly-lit cavernous interior are studded from top to bottom with row upon row of nest-holes, sometimes numbering more than a thousand. The construction is not the same in all dovecotes and the overall impression varies from a rough stone block surface dotted with holes to the more regular striped effect of brick and mortar, or the more hygienic look of whitewashed plaster walls. Further striking variations depend on the arrangement of the orifices, generally in linear or alternate patterns, giving a chequer-board or honeycomb appearance, but occasionally in other groupings.

The resemblance between the interior of many early dovecotes and the pigeons' natural rocky abode has been remarked upon by at least one writer.

> *Man indeed has only taken advantage of certain habits natural to the species and by the substitution of an artificial for a real cavern has...brought it into a kind of voluntary subjection and rendered it subservient to his benefit and use.*

**Early Basic Arrangement**

The fundamental proportions of the birds' nesting recesses were laid down by Varro in Roman times.

> *Each nest should be so constructed as to have an opening large enough to allow only entrance and exit and on the interior should be three palms in all directions. Under each row there should be fixed a board two palms wide to serve as an entrance and walkway.*

These elementary but sensible measurements work out at roughly 12 inches square for the nest, which is less generous than many of those in English dovecotes today and eight inches for the ledge which is wider than is generally found. Later English writers stressed the need for the nests to be large enough and even went so far as to recommend the provision of three or four nests for each two pairs of birds. Accommodation had to be

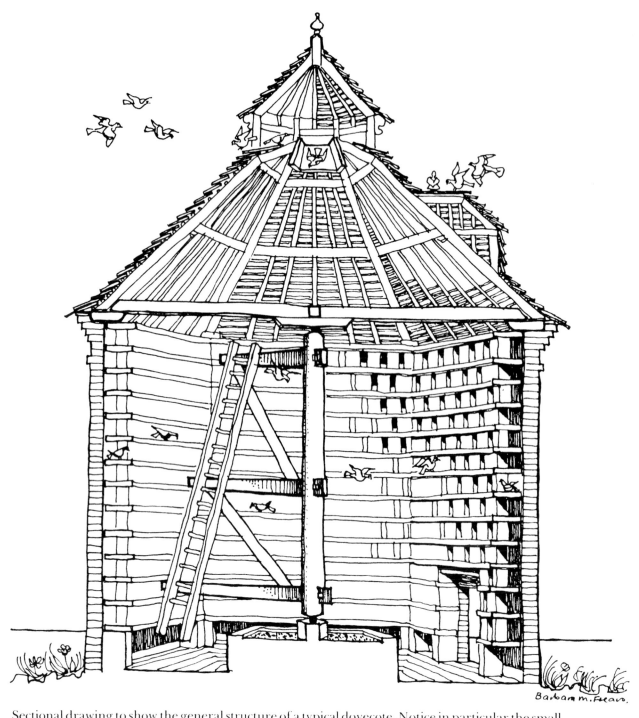

Sectional drawing to show the general structure of a typical dovecote. Notice in particular the small entrance doorway; the thick walls in the form of a double skin to accommodate nesting holes and alighting ledges; a centrally-swivelling potence allowing access to nests at all levels; a dormer window for light and ventilation; and a summit cupola enabling the birds to come and go except when closed by means of a trapdoor.

large enough for at least one parent and two squabs, but was sometimes stretched to the limit when eggs were being incubated by the hen bird at one end and chicks were being fed by the cock at the other. Such was the rapid breeding cycle of the domesticated pigeon.

In this country many of the first nesting places were constructed as simple shafts in the thickness of the wall, sometimes having a rough terminal expansion. Later it became customary to make the interior of the nest L-shaped, partly to allow room for the sitting bird's tail, but also to afford greater seclusion, as one writer puts it 'so that your birds sit dark and private', thus imitating their natural rocky habitat. In several dovecotes, a single L-shaped block of hewn stone forms the front wall of the nest and determines its form. At the Garway dovecote in Here-fordshire, each entrance hole is seven inches square and after extending through the thickness of the walls for 17 inches, turns at a right-angle for 12 inches or so. All the nests in one tier turn in the same direction, those in the rows immediately above and below it being reversed. This alternate arrangement is often found in dovecotes of all ages, but is not invariable. The overall construction is sometimes crude and without a precise angle, but in later examples, the internal masonry or brickwork fits more accurately and often shows a high standard of craftsmanship.

## Construction and Design

By and large, the same building materials were used for exteriors and interiors so that wooden fittings, occasionally with lath and plaster or mud partitions, feature in most half-timbered dovecotes. Matching stone or brick is found in many others, while chalk, clunch, slate, granite, pantiles, cob, and gypsum plaster are also still found. At Willington, Bedfordshire, the soapstone nest construction is probably exceptional. Equally rare is the use of tufa for the niches in the 16th century Ivy Thorn Manor dovecote at Street in Somerset. This lightweight, coarsely porous form of limestone is found in only small deposits in the Mendips but was quarried there in medieval times and is a feature of the vaulted ceilings of the chapter house and lady chapel of Wells Cathedral.

Removable wooden boxes and wicker baskets resting on shelves have been reported, but none appear to have survived. The use of clay pottery for making nests was recommended in the past as being warmer for the birds, but very few examples exist in dovecotes here although they are still common in France and in Mediterranean countries. There are rare examples at Newtimber Place in Sussex where most of the 500 nests are conventionally brick-built, but the top three tiers resemble clay flowerpots laid on their sides and at Snape with Thorpe in Yorkshire, cylindrical terracotta units, believed to date from the 19th century, are fitted in a

*(left)* Interior of restored dovecote from Haselour Hall. There are wooden nest-boxes and the wall-timbering above is now obscured by exterior brick cladding (see also p.143)
*(right)* Wichenford Court showing arched wooden nest-boxes

dovecote of earlier date. In a few districts, pre-formed nesting units of puddled clay or gypsum plaster were built into position, generally with the support of a wooden framework.

There is considerable variation in the shape of nest entrances; square, rectangular, arched, circular and even wedge and ogee shapes are to be found, but the square form predominates. A tiny parapet built across the threshold of some openings at Hawley Manor, Kent, is an unusual feature and may have been intended to prevent squabs from falling out of the nest. In many dovecotes the first row of nest-holes starts about three to four feet from the floor, which is believed to have been a precaution against the threat of climbing marauders, or may be otherwise explained by the pigeons' reluctance to nest near the ground.

Alighting ledges for the birds take several forms. In some dovecotes they are continuous and are placed below each row of nests, while in others they are less generously fitted to alternate rows or are even more widely spaced. In a few interiors of later date, individual landing stages made of stone, or one or two bricks placed end-on are used. At Weston House, Albury, Surrey, the recently restored octagonal brick dovecote contains both single and continuous craggy ironstone ledges. A cruder arrangement is to be seen in the ancient dovecote at Hurley in Berkshire, where a few rough pieces of stone, inserted at random, are the only provision for alighting. In those dovecotes without ledges or perches of any kind, the presence of deep claw marks on the brick or stone bear testimony to the poor birds' difficulties in getting into their nests. Rarely, as at Tattershall Castle, a wooden rod is fitted below each hole, while in Nottinghamshire, oak pegs forming part of the interior wooden framework are still to be seen at the Cromwell dovecote.

*(left)* Tattershall Castle showing lath and plaster nest-boxes with unusual perching rods
*(right)* Large central nest-bearing column within Fairford dovecote

51

Several ingenious ways of increasing wall space were used in order to maximize the number of nests in the dovecote. The simple partition wall in large two-chambered structures is relatively common, but the arrangement at Notley Abbey dovecote is extremely unusual. Here, four tall projecting piers attached to the centre of each internal wall carry between them an additional 400 nests, almost doubling the capacity. Although this may be unique in England, the dovecote at Leitcheston at Moray in Scotland has a somewhat similar construction. The centre of the interior was also exploited for extra accommodation as in the large circular dovecote at Fairford, Gloucestershire, where a substantial tall column provides over 200 additional nests. Other central blocks are to be found at Shenton Hall, Leicestershire; at Chicheley, Buckinghamshire and at Whitton Hall, Shropshire, in each of which the base of a potence is inserted. In the hexagonal dovecote at Shapwick House, Somerset, the six foot central stone table of matching shape contains 72 nests.

## Labour-saving Devices

Ledges and nest-holes were often used as footholds for those climbing up to collect squabs and eggs, but a clever contrivance known as a potence, from the French term meaning a gallows, represented an early attempt to save labour. These contraptions lent themselves best to circular dovecotes and several are still to be found intact. Each potence consists of a stout wooden pole or tree trunk placed centrally and pivoted above and below; one or two ladders are attached to its lateral arms and the whole assembly rotates to provide convenient access to the nests at all levels. The potence at Dunster in Somerset is said to be 400 years old and still moves at the touch of a finger. Although originally designed to fit circular dovecotes, potences were occasionally fitted in others of less suitable shape. There is a well-preserved example in the square dovecote at Westington Old Manor, Gloucestershire, where the out-of-reach corners are straddled by beams which afford footholds for access. Another adaptation is to be seen at Fyfield Manor, Wiltshire, where the square interior has been rounded off at the corners.

An uncommon, possibly unique substitution for a potence, in the large square dovecote at Penmon Priory, Anglesey, consists of a broad central stone column with projecting steps spirally disposed, from which all nests can be reached.

A completely different method of access to the nests inside square and rectangular dovecotes, utilises a framework of wooden scaffolding. It is made up of a number of beams fitted close to the walls which provide walkways at two or three levels and these are connected with each other by ladders. Remains of such scaffolds are to be found in the outsize two-

*(top)* Interior of Frampton Court
dovecote with potence
(see also p.194)
*(bottom left)* Notley Abbey. Note
elaborate roof timbers and one of
four accessory piers to increase
nesting capacity (see also p.141)
*(bottom right)* Trellis-work wooden
nest-boxes at Pump House Farm
(see also p.114)

chambered dovecote at Willington, Bedfordshire; in the large square brick example at South Stoke Farm, Oxfordshire; and on a smaller scale at Lee Farm, Sussex. By contrast, the structure at Hawley Manor, Kent, is in excellent repair and today it is still possible to use the peg-ladders and walkways.

The elaborate roof timbering in many dovecotes is strikingly visible from inside. Although relatively crude, the construction is often impressive in its ruggedness and ingenuity of design. Some roofs have been renewed, but others still retain their original stout beams and rafters, often of oak, together with their massive doorway lintels. Circular dovecotes are sometimes fitted with simple crossed tie beams at roof springer level, an arrangement which was intended to provide the upper pivot of a potence. A few roofs of the larger circular cotes have an intricate pattern of annular and post supports as at Avebury in Wiltshire and Halswell House, Somerset.

## Running the Dovecote

Collecting eggs and squabs by means of potence or scaffold was more or less straightforward, although it no doubt caused much commotion in the dovecote. In order to reduce the general upheaval, such tasks were generally undertaken early in the day when many of the birds were out foraging. The rule that anyone entering the dovecote should knock three or four times beforehand is easily understood. It was intended

> *...to allow those birds which are shyest time to fly away instead of making them dash about the interior in alarm, raising a great commotion and dust, injuring themselves, frightening any quieter birds that may happen to be incubating and probably causing numerous desertions afterwards.*
>
> (Sebastian Delamer, 1854)

Catching adult birds, either for periodic culling of the older breeding stock or on a large scale for the shooting matches of the 18th and 19th centuries, involved the use of a long-handled net wielded from the floor and was a completely different exercise. It was often a nocturnal pursuit when the birds were roosting and the resulting disturbance can be imagined. As a preliminary, it was clearly necessary to close all means of exit; the glover or cupola was shut by an inner trapdoor, operated by pulley and cord either from within the dovecote or sometimes from outside, or was reached by ladder from the upper stages. Windows or other openings in the walls were generally closed by external shutters or netting impaled on spikes, a few remnants of which are still to be found.

Management of the dovecote was not particularly labour-intensive, although a whole-time keeper of the pigeons has been noted in the distant past. Apart from the need for daily feeding, occasional cleaning and whitewashing, and egg and squab collection, little custodial care was required because, once settled in the dovecote, the pigeons' inborn homing instinct ensured their return to the nest each evening and removed the need for invigilation. However, certain routine tasks for the month of January were laid down in an early rhyming calendar of husbandry:

> *Feed Doves but kill not*
> *If loose them ye will not*
> *Dove house repair*
> *Make douve hole fair*
> *For hop ground cold*
> *Douve doong worth gold.*
> (Thomas Tusser, 1580)

A remarkable feature of these dovecote communities was the ability of large numbers of birds to live together harmoniously in a confined space. In fact, domesticated pigeons preferred a communal existence and their ceaseless preoccupation with breeding left little time for serious squabbling. Furthermore, the birds by nature pursue a well-ordered existence and the dovecote flock followed an exemplary routine of rising at daybreak and roosting without fail at dusk or earlier.

Some owners left the birds to forage in the countryside and only fed them when snow lay on the ground. Others supplemented their diet daily with dried grain and vetches of various sorts, such as wheat, barley, peas, beans, lentils, hemp and millet. In the past, several varieties of pea and bean were grown as field crops in due rotation, the coarser varieties being much used to feed horses, pigeons and the poor. Although pigeons prefer dried grain and pulses, they show remarkable adaptability if left to themselves and will eat a mixed diet of snails, grubs, insects and worms as well as grass, weed seeds and even green vegetation. In those city parks with oak trees, the birds have even been seen eating acorns.

It was, of course, in the general interest to maintain a well-fed flock, not only for effective breeding, but also to encourage the birds to stay at home. In addition, it may have been considered likely that adequately nourished pigeons would cause less damage to surrounding crops and gardens. In many households the birds' food was sprinkled outside the dovecote at a fixed time each day, but in bad weather it was sometimes put inside at the base of the walls which was considered to be the cleanest place. However, there is no evidence that interior troughs supplied from outside hoppers, as used by the Romans, were ever installed in England. Neither was their practice of force-feeding the squabs with masticated bread adopted here.

It is to be hoped that the cruel Roman practice of breaking the squabs' legs to keep them in the nest while being fattened was never carried out.

Water is a vital requirement for the birds, not only for drinking and bathing, but it is also essential for the secretion of 'pigeon's milk' with which the parents feed their young. Apart from the rare interior water trough at Garway in Herefordshire, water was seldom provided inside the dovecote, but an outside source was generally located close at hand.


## Enticement, Protection and Superstition

In the past, much effort was expended in ensuring that the birds would not desert their own dovecote and various ploys and enticements were used to make them 'love the dovehouse more'. Sometimes, there seems to have been an element of competition involved as it was not unknown for dovecote owners to try and lure away their neighbours' pigeons. In stocking a new dovecote there was often some difficulty in persuading the birds to settle down permanently; they are capricious creatures and liable to desert a new home for another. Being gregarious by nature, they prefer the crowded environment of an established community. In the 18th century, Gilbert White of Selborne described the problem besetting Sir Roger Mostyn who lived near Llandudno in Gwynedd where his house doves

> ...though tempted by plenty of food and gentle treatment can never be prevailed on to inhabit their cote for any time: but as soon as they begin to breed, betake themselves to the fastness of Ormeshead and deposit their young in safety amidst the inaccessible caverns and precipices of that stupendous promontory.

It was therefore customary to confine pairs of birds within a new cote until the first brood had been hatched, in order to form a firm bond to their home. Another measure was to purchase the birds from a distant source, even across the Channel, to lessen the possibility that they might return to their birthplace.

Apart from these sensible precautions, several inducements, some ancient and some decidedly peculiar, were used to bind the birds to their home. Various herbs and spices were not only hung around the door and scattered inside the dovecote, but were also applied to the birds themselves. Cumin seeds, which have a pungent smell, seem to have been much used, but rosemary, lavender, rue, frankincense and myrrh have also been mentioned. Fumigation was also recommended with asafoetida, a native plant of Persia and Afghanistan, which was popular in Roman times and is still employed in the East. It is derived from a variety of giant fennel and

56

has a ghastly smell likened to bad garlic. Extracts prepared from the milky juice of the plant are today incorporated in some of the remedies of alternative medicine.

A more soundly-based edible enticement was the much quoted 'salt-cat', the expression deriving from a contraction of 'cate' meaning a delicacy. There were many recipes for this concoction, but it consisted basically of a sort of cake made up of lime, grit and salt which are essential mineral requirements of the bird and are still provided by competent owners today. If deprived of these substances the pigeons have been known to peck at the mortar on walls and roofs. As with other birds, lime is needed to harden the eggshell and grit aids the digestion, but the pigeon's singular love of salt may date back to the time when its ancestors fed on the seashore. In contrast, there can be no rational explanation for the 'dogge roasted' which was prescribed in earliest times as a great attraction. This involved killing and disembowelling the animal, which was then stuffed with cumin seed and roasted in sweet wine and honey. Another unsavoury and equally superstitious idea was to mix the boiled head and feet of a goat into an unpleasant mess which the birds were said to like.

In addition to these persuasions there was also the worry of protecting the dovecote birds from marauders among whom have been numbered rats, cats, weasels, squirrels, ferrets, owls, hawks, starlings and the rarer polecats and pine martens. In the 18th century the brown or Hanoverian rat arrived in this country; described as 'the new invader from abroad', it was regarded as having superior agility and determination compared with the older English black rat and as being a serious new threat to the cote.

*(left)* Stoke-sub-Hamdon Priory dovecote. The roofless ruin clearly reveals the early crude stone construction (see also p.227)
*(right)* Coombe Place. High quality construction, chiefly of whitewashed brickwork, separated by chalk alighting ledges (see also p.153)

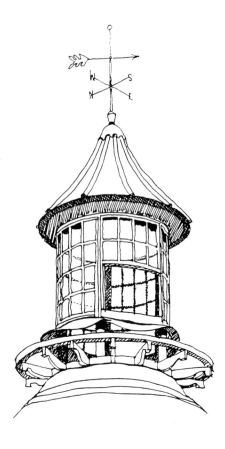

Over the ages several measures, some sensible, some irrational, were advocated for dealing with all these creatures. The recommendation by Palladius in the 4th century to encircle the building with a mechanical barrier of prickly gorse and briars might have discouraged some intruders. A very different method of dealing with one particular menace was described by Samuel Pepys:

> *To Dr Williams who did carry me into his garden...and did show me a dog that he hath do kill all the cats that come hither to kill his pigeons and do afterwards bury them and do it with so much care that they shall be quite covered, that if the tip of the tail hangs out, he will take up the cat again and dig the hole deeper which is very strange: and he tells me that he do believe that he hath killed 100 cats.*

Could it be a tall story? Other writers mention dogs being tethered outside dovecotes, presumably to scare away all unwelcome visitors.

Other deterrents were founded more on ancient myth and magic. A curious charm against weasels was to hang up inside the dovecote the rope with which a man had been hanged; the wolf or stag's head similarly displayed must have been equally ineffective! An even more bizarre ritual in which sealed earthenware jars containing live or mummified young kestrels were buried beneath the dovecote floor or hung up on the inner walls was described by Pliny and was still being advocated in 16th century England. The practice probably stemmed from a custom in ancient Egypt where falcons were offered up to the falcon-god, Horus, Lord of the Sky. Thousands of pottery jars containing the birds' remains are still to be found today in underground vaults and galleries near Cairo. These ritual offerings may have symbolised a plea to the god for protection and good fortune; a sentiment echoed millenia later by dovecote owners, but possibly with the threat of predatory hawks in mind.

All this simply serves to illustrate the lengths to which people were prepared to go in order to nurture and protect the flock.

# CHAPTER V

# First Dovecotes in
# England and Wales

### Integral Nests

There is no record of dovecotes in the Domesday Book (1086) which supports the general view that the Normans introduced domestication of the pigeon to this country. There is an absence of any reference to the custom in the Dark Ages between the Romans and the Normans, but it seems quite possible that the Anglo-Saxons kept culvers in crude culver-houses. The very earliest provision of housing for the bird is to be found in the castles of the Norman barons. Excellent examples of integral nests can still be seen in the stone-built keeps of Rochester Castle, Kent (1126) and Conisborough Castle, Yorkshire (1180). At Rochester, the nest-holes are situated within the three top turrets of the square keep and also in several rows along the top of its south-facing inner wall. At Conisborough, the six see page 66 buttresses of the massive circular keep project upwards beyond the crest of the parapet. Each one is hollowed out on its inner face and these six spaces were used to house two water-tanks, an oven, two watchtowers and a pigeon house in which several flight-holes can still be seen on the exterior walls. In each castle the number of pigeon nests is relatively small, about a hundred, which would not have provided a very useful contribution to the kitchen pot on a regular basis, but might have been a vital source of meat in a siege. Or perhaps the birds were intended to be used as messengers in such an event? Reports of this custom in peace and war must have been fresh in the minds of warriors returning from the early Crusades.

The keep formed the domestic core of the castle, a dwelling house in the inconvenient but necessary form of a tower. Either permanently or as an emergency stronghold it contained accommodation for eating and sleeping, together with a chapel for spiritual welfare. The roof platform and parapet provided the fighting deck. This defensive pattern of domestic architecture continued for several centuries, long after the need for a garrison or stronghold had gone. It was adopted by Ralph Cromwell, the Lord Treasurer of England in the 15th century at Tattershall Castle, Lincolnshire. This enormous square red brick keep, now splendidly restored, was planned from the beginning as a grand mansion. The four large corner turrets contain garderobes on each floor except one which serves as an integral dovecote and is lined with wattle and daub nests for hundreds of birds.

Early surviving integral nests are not all located in keeps. At Bodiam Castle, Kent (1385), rows of stone hewn recesses are to be found high up on the inner wall of the south-west drum tower. They are sited immediately above the kitchen and would seem to have been a handy source of food. Nowadays the tower is roofless and devoid of floors, so there is nothing left between the pigeon-holes at the top and the ten foot deep castle well, below.

Early references throw light on the widespread existence of specially built pigeon-holes within the fabric of medieval parish churches. In some cases the birds were the perquisites of the incumbent, as recorded in 1375: 'At an augmentation of the vicarage of Kingston-upon-Thames, it was agreed by the impropriating monastery that the vicar should have the pigeons or other birds bred in the church or chapels'. Later accounts refer to birds being common church property and shared among the parishioners.

Nowadays, nesting places are still to be found in a few churches occupying either one storey of the church tower or the roof space above the chancel. At the 13th century church of St Mary's, Sarnesfield, in Herefordshire, the later west tower contains 100 holes in the middle stage below the belfry. A similar situation is found in the towers of several other churches such as those of St James, Birlingham, Worcestershire; St Peter, Upton, in Nottinghamshire; and St Andrew, Collingbourne Ducis in Wiltshire. Entry-holes for the birds were provided in the outer walls and a staircase from the main body of the church gave access for the custodian. Pigeons are particularly sensitive to loud and sudden noise, so it is surprising that they could be persuaded to settle in such close proximity to the bells. Presumably, they became accustomed in time to the intermittent disturbance.

see page 66 The original crossing tower of the Norman church of St John at Elkstone in Gloucestershire, collapsed in the 13th century and the remaining walls of its base above the chancel were built up in 1400 into a dovecote which contains 40 nest-holes on two walls, others having been blocked off. A lancet-shaped opening, now glazed, in the east wall gave access for the birds. At St Faith's church, Overbury in Worcestershire, a larger number of 200 nests occupy the space between the groined ceiling of the chancel and the roof proper. Integral nesting places were also provided in other convenient locations such as the porches and gatehouses of the larger abbey and priory churches. At Tewkesbury Abbey in Gloucestershire, for example, they have been found in the room above the north porch, which dates from Norman times.

60

### Freestanding Dovecotes in Castles

The first freestanding dovecotes were built as appendages to Norman castles. They evolved as a practical extension of the interior arrangement and several are still extant. In construction they are rugged stone rotundas which derived distantly from the large tortoise or beehive-shaped *columbaria* of the Romans and established the circular pattern. Their domed, corbelled roofs have an *oculus* or central opening at the summit, which admits light and air and enables the birds to come and go. The small doorways with stout wooden doors at ground level are crudely constructed, but a few show interesting features. The unusual ogee-headed doorway at Kinwarton in Warwickshire is beautifully preserved and provides a useful clue to its 14th century origin. At Garway, an arch of crudely-shaped *voussoir* or wedge-shaped stones is set at a distance above the lintel both within and without; on the outside, the space between the lintel and the arch carries an inscription naming the builder and his date. A strikingly similar form of construction is to be found hundreds of miles away at its contemporary counterpart at Hurley in Berkshire.

The massive windowless vertical rubblestone walls, in the thickness of which the nests were built, are sometimes encircled by one or more string courses to deter marauding, climbing creatures such as rats, cats and weasels. Their whole appearance is solid and impregnable, more like forts than farm buildings and they look well able to have withstood the ravages of time and the incursions of all predators, both human and animal.

A few of the very ancient castle dovecotes have survived unaltered chiefly in the western part of the country. In southern Pembrokeshire the impressive remains of the 12th century Manorbier Castle stand in seclusion above the sea and sand dunes. It has been described as the most complete example of the 'Welsh baronial' complex with its curtain walls, gatehouse, mill, fishponds, park and dovecote, much of which remains. The castle was built in the 12th and 13th centuries during the first Norman expedition into Wales. The well-known scholar, monk, traveller and chronicler, Gerald of Wales was born there in 1146. The dovecote stands alone on the seaward side of the castle outside the walls beside the site of the old fishpond, its roof now capped with vegetation. Across the peninsula from Manorbier at Angle there are remains of a square stone defensive tower built in 1215, which is situated strategically at the southern entrance to Milford Haven. The nearby circular, domed dovecote is believed to be contemporaneous and is still complete and in fair condition. Like Manorbier, it possesses the unusual feature of having flight-holes in the main walls, which is only found elsewhere in the manorial dovecote at Cadoxton Court, Glamorgan, and a few of the ancient beehive dovecotes of Cornwall and Devon.

Dunster Castle, on a hill overlooking the Bristol Channel in Somerset, see page 67

(left) Ancient stone 'beehive' dovecote at Angle, near southern entrance to Milford Haven, probably 13th century
(right) Van, near Caerphilly. Another early example which collapsed after a severe winter in 1947

was built by the Norman Baron de Bohun soon after the Conquest and the circular stone dovecote which stands some distance away probably dates from the same time. However, it was subsequently altered in 1150 by the prior and monks sent from the Benedictine abbey in Bath to build the church. The original roof was replaced much later with the present conical one. Nevertheless it remains a fine and much-quoted example of its type.

In the eastern counties the earliest surviving dovecotes of similar design are the two which are situated east and west of Allington Castle in Kent. They are claimed to be 12th century in origin. One of the pair is now a roofless ruin, but its interior nesting places are well preserved. The other dovecote was converted into an attractive cottage in 1907 by Lord Conway, while he was restoring the castle. It now has a conical tiled roof superimposed upon a massively thick stone dome which may well be original.

On the Gower peninsula in South Wales there are two other castles with circular dovecotes of later date which deserve mention. At Penrice the large 16th century dovecote is built against the curtain wall and is in a fair state of preservation. At Oxwich the partially ruined dovecote stands at an angle between two ranges of the castle, its square interior nest-holes now strikingly visible from outside. At Baron Fitzscrob's Castle in Herefordshire there are several tiers remaining in an excavated dovecote which is claimed to have been added to the Norman castle in medieval times.

## Abbeys and Priories

The religious life of the country was greatly influenced by the Norman Conquest. It stimulated an increase in the number of monks in existing monasteries and the foundation of many more establishments including priories, churches, monastic granges and farms and rectories. The feudal barons, the new possessors of vast castles and estates could well afford to be financially generous towards religious orders of their choosing which greatly helped the different orders to flourish at this period. However, after the long French wars of the 12th century and the Black Death in the 14th century, religious life fell into decline and fewer communities thrived.

In medieval times the church was a dominant power in English life. The monasteries, apart from being great spiritual and cultural centres were also the largest landowners in the country, at one time being said to own a quarter of the entire land. Their large estates were well-managed and intensively farmed and furthermore the religious fraternity enjoyed the great advantage, not shared by the barons and their warlike followers, of having plenty of time to keep accurate accounts of their land and property and to study the management of their stock. The first treatise on English agriculture, *The Book of Husbandry*, which was written by Walter of Henley in the 13th century for the monks of Canterbury, contains sound economic advice for any landowner and illustrates the importance attached to dovecotes at that time: 'Survey your lands and tenements by true and sworn men. First survey your courts, gardens, dovehouses, curtilages, what they are yearly beyond the valuation.'

Surviving monastic chronicles, inquisitions, rolls and other documents provide invaluable sources of information about day-to-day lives of the times. There is plenty of documentary evidence referring to columbaria being owned by many abbeys and monasteries as well as their granges and farms. For example, seven dovecotes were built for the priory of Dunstable between 1248 and 1273, while the Evesham Chronicles record that four dovecotes belonged to the abbey manor farms. The abbot at Croyland Abbey in Lincolnshire is reported to have possessed two dovecotes in the 14th century, the birds from which were eaten by the brethren in the abbey: in addition, some were given as a reward for services, some went to Court Sessions and others were used as exchange in kind. The same document mentions that in 1322, three pigeons cost one penny, a not inconsiderable sum in those days. In the chronicles of the monastery of St Albans it is recorded that a new pigeon-house had been built, the birds from which were customarily divided among the brethren, but others were given to the poor. An inventory in York dated 1281-1372 quotes the value of a dovecote as being £6.13s.4d which apparently worked out at half that of a watermill: by comparison, a sheep-house was valued at £3.6s.4d and a

63

brew-house at £5.0s.0d. It is quite clear that dovecotes counted as substantial material assets. Closer to the domestic scene is a description by the Bishop of Exeter following his visit in the 14th century to the Augustinian priory of Launceston in Cornwall. He found that each canon in residence possessed not only a chamber of his own but a page, a kitchen garden, a dovecote and a dog.

Several dovecotes belonging to the various religious orders are still to be found in different parts of the country, but chiefly those which were attached to their outlying units, such as monastic granges and farms which supplied provender to the parent house. Provision for the physical as well as the spiritual welfare of large monastery households, together with the obligation to give victuals to paying-guests and numerous travellers, made great demands on the larder.

Some orders, such as the Benedictines, were busy over here even before the Conquest. St Edmundsbury at Bury St Edmunds was founded by King Canute between 1017 and 1035 and was one of the most powerful and wealthy Benedictine monasteries in the country. Nowadays, apart from the gatehouse, there is very little remaining above ground, but the foundations and lower walls of two dovecotes have been identified. A large polygonal one stood against the outer wall and a circular one was situated next to the abbot's house alongside the stables, brew-house, bakery and kitchen. Unfortunately there are no firm dates for either dovecote.

There is a curious sequence of events connected with the ruins of the dovecote belonging to the Augustinian priory at Llanthony in Gwent, both of which were built between 1180 and 1220. The existence of the dovecote was discovered accidentally in 1907 by workmen digging for building stone to construct a new road. The ensuing archaeological study demonstrated circular walls containing characteristic nesting places of what was assumed to be an unusual subterranean *columbarium*. The report at that time failed to explain the reason for a dovecote being built underground. However, a recent survey and further excavation in 1979 has shown convincingly that the remains are those of a typical dovecote which had become buried over the centuries. Now that the floor and lower part of the walls are clearly revealed, today's workers are unable to refrain from commenting that the earlier concept of a subterranean construction was 'an uncharacteristically ill thought-out observation'. Their description also revealed the general layout of the outlying buildings of the priory. The inner court contained the fishponds, the brew-house and the poultry yard while the outer court housed the barn and various stock enclosures for cattle and sheep. The dovecote was situated beside the infirmary rather than in the more common position beside the barn and granary.

see page 68

At the site of the long-vanished Benedictine priory of Hurley in Berkshire, founded in 1086, an excellent circular buttressed dovecote, dated 1307, still stands beside the tithe barn. The walls are

Dovecote within tufa monolith, Cappadocia

*(top)* Pigeon-holes in battlements of Conisborough Castle
*(bottom)* Remaining nest-holes above chancel of St John's church, Elkstone

66

*(top)* Knights Hospitallers dovecote at Quenington
*(bottom)* Norman dovecote at Dunster

Priory dovecote, Hurley

68

Earliest dated dovecote, at Garway, with later cupola

Much altered 14th century dovecote at Kinwarton

Early crude manorial cote at Blackford House

13th Century dovecote at Cadoxton Court

72

characteristically massive, measuring almost four feet in thickness and the four buttresses reach the full height of the walls. The cone-shaped roof is a subsequent replacement. Also in Berkshire there is a later 14th-15th century circular example standing on the site of Bisham Abbey which was founded by the Knights Templars, but became an Augustinian priory in 1337. The thick walls are built of chalk clunch with unusual flat red tiles between the rough coursing. At Daglingworth Manor in Gloucestershire, the circular dovecote which is in excellent order is believed to be the only surviving building of a cell of the once famous Benedictine nunnery at Godstow in Oxfordshire, founded in 1133.

## Knights Templars and Hospitallers

The two orders of that extraordinary international brotherhood of highly-born military monks were founded in Jerusalem in the 12th century, largely to provide lodging and protection for pilgrims on their way to and from the Holy Land. Later, they established hospices for the poor, sick and aged in this country and in France. Over here, one of the most important houses of the Knights Templars was on the Welsh border at Garway in Herefordshire, but after their persecution and suppression it see page 69 was transferred at the end of the 13th century to the Knights Hospitallers, also known as the Knights of St John. The magnificent ancient dovecote with its original domed roof still stands unchanged today alongside the chapel of the Order. It has been repeatedly quoted as being the oldest dovecote in the country, but this claim is misleading. It is probably the earliest, unaltered and authentically-dated example according to a barely legible inscription over the door which, translated from the Latin, reads: 'In the year 1326 Brother Richard built this dovecote'. However, several original dovecotes in Wales and the West Country are almost certainly older. Another possession of the Knights of St John is the village of Rosemarket in Pembrokeshire which, together with its mill and some land, was granted to them in the 13th century. It was probably used as an outlying farm and the dovecote, of a similar type to those at Manorbier and Angle, but much smaller, still stands.

At the site of a preceptory of the Knights Hospitallers at Quenington in see page 67 Gloucestershire, little remains except the gatehouse and the circular stone dovecote which may be the one mentioned by Prior Philip de Thame in a letter to the Grand Master, Elyan de Villanove, in 1338. Its thick walls and the two slit windows, widely splayed within, proclaim its early date.

The hospital of St Cross at Winchester was founded in 1136 by Henry de Blois, Bishop of Winchester, to accommodate 13 'poor, impotent men' and to provide dinners daily for another 100, increased later to 200, poor men. It was under the control of the Knights Hospitallers from 1185 onwards.

An engraving of 1774 showing the circular dovecote which once served the hospital of St Cross, Winchester

Nowadays, only the sacristy of the early building remains, but an 18th century engraving shows a circular dovecote in the foreground which was probably built as late as the 15th century.

**Monastic Granges and Farms**

In addition to having dovecotes on the premises, many abbeys and monasteries maintained others on their outlying granges and farms, which were often situated at a considerable distance from the parent house. The grange of Abbots Llantwit in South Glamorgan belonged to the Benedictines of Tewkesbury Abbey, who were granted the land in 1100. The buildings of this grange originally occupied three fields, one of which is still called Dovecote Field, but today only the 13th century gatehouse, dovecote and part of the barn remain. The stone dovecote is very similar to those already mentioned at Manorbier, Angle and Garway. Another surviving round dovecote stands in isolation on the site of a moated grange see page 70 at Kinwarton in Warwickshire, which belonged to the Benedictines of Evesham Abbey. It is believed to be 14th century in origin, but has been much altered over the years and the exterior is now rendered. It is in the custodianship of the National Trust. The Evesham Benedictines also possessed a dovecote three miles away at Hillborough Manor, Temple Grafton; this large, squat building has a diameter of 24 feet and contains 900 niches of construction similar to those of Kinwarton.

**Rectories**

From earliest times, rectories were provided with farmland to support the parish priests, most of whom were said to be part-time farmers in the Middle Ages. Together with abbots and lords of the manor they also

74

Artist's reconstruction of the monastic grange enclave at Abbots Llantwit

enjoyed the privilege of possessing a dovecote and used the birds for their own table and to provide for the numerous wayside travellers whom they were obliged to feed. Sometimes a dovecote was rented in exchange for a tithe payment. At Tintagel in Cornwall, a massive round tower of slate stone with a slate roof still stands close to the vicarage. Local legend relates that it was originally part of a monastic building belonging to the abbey of Fontrevault and probably dates from 1259. Several other rectorial dovecotes of later date are still to be found, amongst which is a fine circular stone example in the grounds of the former vicarage at West Camel in Somerset.

## Manors

It seems from the records that few landowners, great or small, failed to exercise their prerogative to build dovecotes. A description, written in 1289, of the manor of Feering in Essex shows that the dovecote occupied pride of place along with the chapel within the courtyard. Estate Books show that the Lords Berkeley of the 12th century Berkeley Castle in Gloucestershire had a dovecote upon each of their manors and on almost every farmstead; from one dovecote alone they derived more than 2,000 pigeons annually. Unfortunately, none of these cotes has survived, but there are a few remaining on manorial estates elsewhere. On the site of the 13th century fortified manor house of Cadoxton Court on the Gower peninsula, now replaced by a later mansion, there stands a splendid see page 72

75

dovecote which is believed to be contemporary with the original house. It has a domed roof and thick walls pierced by several through holes in its lower half. Three string courses encircle the upper wall and roof. It has recently been restored.

see page 71

At Blackford House in Somerset, the rugged sandstone dovecote is thought to date from the time when William the Conqueror's nephew built a manor on the site, which was destroyed by fire in the 19th century. Unlike the Norman dovecote at Dunster Castle nearby, its original corbelled, domed roof is well preserved. The summit *oculus* is now glazed and, in addition to the 300 nests, two tiers of eight widely-separated square holes occupy the inner surface of the dome; these are very uncommon, possibly unique features. Are they extra nesting places or blocked flight-holes?

The dovecote at Charleston Manor in East Sussex is also probably of Norman origin. It is thought to be coeval with the original 12th century manor, parts of which are incorporated in the present house.

In Cornwall, at the manor of Cotehele, there is an ancient beehive stone dovecote with three encircling string courses, which is thought to date from 1353 when the house was built. Both are under the care of the National Trust. Also in this county at Bussow Vean, Trevanion and Crafthole there are ancient manorial dovecotes of 13th and 14th century origin, which have six to twelve through flight-holes in their walls. This feature, which is found in some of the other dovecotes in South Wales already mentioned, also occurs in dovecotes at Bigbury and Hardwick in Devon. In general, the early Cornish cotes are considerably smaller than their Welsh counterparts and contain nesting places for only 100-200 birds. The example at Bussow, built of granite, has such a primitive appearance that it has been taken for a prehistoric dwelling.

Although manor houses were dominant features of the landscape from the 13th century onwards, countless numbers have disappeared together with hosts of medieval villages. Many dovecotes have met a similar fate, but for a time some of them outlasted the parent house. This observation was made by William Cobbett writing in *Rural Rides* of his travels along the Avon Valley in Hampshire, early in the 19th century:

> *Every parish had its manor house in the first place: and then there were down this valley, twenty-one others: so that in the distance of about thirty miles, there stood fifty mansion houses. Where are they now? I believe there are but eight that are at all worthy of the name. In several places, I saw, still remaining, indubitable traces of an ancient manor house, namely a dovecote or pigeon house. The poor pigeons have kept possession of their heritage from generation to generation...*

Today there are no dovecotes left at all in the district that he described.

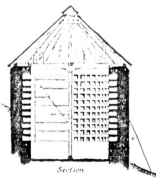

*Section*

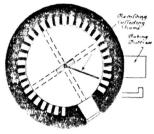

*Revolving Collecting Frame*

*Raking Buttress*

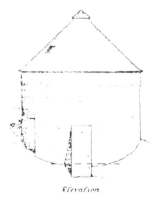

*Elevation*

CHARLSTON MANOR
- WEST DEAN -

*13th Century Columbarium*

*Plan*

*Scale of Feet*

Surviving Cornish and Devon dovecotes: *(top left)* Pridhamsleigh;
*(top right)* Crafthole; *(bottom left)* Tintagel; *(bottom right)* Bussow Vean

## Sites

The positions of early dovecotes, whether belonging to castle, monastery, manor or farm, varied greatly. Some stand quite alone at a distance from the main building, often near the fishponds, while others are closer and even abut the walls. Occasionally the dovecote was built within the cloister or garth of the abbey or monastery. In early medieval times, in an attempt to restrict damage to the crops by the marauding birds, pigeon houses were sometimes built on common or wasteland at as great a distance as possible from the cultivated fields. The reverse was later established in France and Scotland where the law decreed that accommodation had to be built well within the owner's land in an attempt to confine the birds' damage to his own crops.

Dovecotes belonging to early farms and granges were generally grouped together with other buildings and were often placed beside the barn and granary. Records from the 13th and 14th century of the home farm at Cuxham in Oxfordshire, which belonged to Merton College, lists the barns, cattle-sheds, stables, carthouse, hayhouse, strawhouse, henhouse and dovecote which surrounded the yard.

According to writers on husbandry in post-medieval times, several factors were important in choosing the best site for the pigeon house. A conspicuous position, free from surrounding trees, was thought to be desirable, not only because the dovecote would be clearly visible to the homing birds, but also because the sound of wind in the trees, like other loud and unusual noises was believed to unsettle them. Nowadays many surviving dovecotes, particularly those which are disused and neglected, have become enveloped by trees and climbing plants, but it is evident that originally they would have stood free from vegetation. Clearly, the pigeons were regarded as nervous and capricious creatures who were liable to desert their home for good if badly upset. The noise from trees was not the only source of disturbance to be avoided: as one writer puts it, 'out of the noise of folks, the dashing of trees one against another and the roaring of waters'.

Shelter from either the prevailing or the bitter east wind was another consideration in siting the dovecote; entrance holes in the walls were often made to face south because the birds love to feel the warmth of the sun as much as they dislike the cold. A source of water in which they could drink and bathe was believed to be essential. It is true that pigeons need an abundant supply, particularly before their annual moult in the autumn; poultry by contrast require very little. For this reason many dovecotes were situated beside monastery and manor fishponds and next to farmyard ponds. The aquatic position at Sundridge Place, Kent, where the dovecote stands in the middle of a lake was an extreme variation.

After the village fields had become enclosed in the 17th century, many

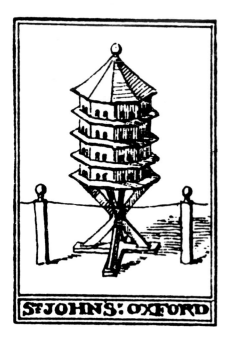

St JOHN'S: OXFORD

farm buildings were grouped in neatly-planned layouts, sometimes arranged around three or four sides of a courtyard; later, riding stables frequently followed this pattern. Dovecotes, either full height or as upper storey lofts were often incorporated in these ranges of buildings and occasionally they occupied the centre of the yard. Although the open situation for dovecotes was still being advocated in the 18th century, another school of thought endorsed this position: 'None is more proper than the middle of a courtyard' and several designs for new dovecotes illustrate the arrangement. Johannes Kip's 1712 engraving of Sherborne Park, Gloucestershire, shows the octagonal stone dovecote in a meadow at some distance from the main building, but today it stands within a courtyard beside the stable block. Pevsner suggests that it was moved when the stables and coachyard were built in 1750. Is this likely?

A few other dovecotes are still to be found in a central position as at Chillington Park, Staffordshire and at Kennel Farm, Amersham. The attractive square dovecote in the stable yard at Cornwell Manor in Oxfordshire is a more modest example, while at Loxley Hall in Staffordshire the surrounding courtyard buildings have completely disappeared, but the octagonal brick dovecote in the middle was saved from demolition at the last moment. At Hothfield Place in Kent, the spacious courtyard, of which one range comprises a dovecote and adjacent stables, is all that remains of the mansion and outliers designed by James Wyatt. In addition to these enclosed yards there are several linear groups of outlying buildings which incorporate a dovecote as at Cosgrove Hall in Northamptonshire.

Finally, the preoccupation with security dictated that wherever possible the dovecote itself, but particularly the entrance door, should be within sight of the main house 'because the master of the family may keep in awe those who go in or come out'.

Dovecotes were not always confined to rural situations; there are a few fragments and some records of urban examples. Documents show that in the 14th century the fourth Lord Berkeley endowed a chapel in Bristol in memory of his mother with property in the city which included 'an house before the gate of St Augustine's monastery with the garden and dovehouse thereof'. Remains of another medieval example have recently been revealed during archaeological excavations at Dorchester, Dorset. The original circular dovecote was of considerable size and the walls were found to contain Roman building materials.

There is also plenty of documentary evidence to show that most Cambridge colleges maintained dovecotes on their premises as well as on their farms. In the accounts of King's Hall dated 1414 an entry appears as 'expenses of the dovehouse'. Corpus Christi College built their dovecote in 1547 and covered the cost by selling some of the church plate. At Trinity Hall the dovecote was evidently still in use in 1730 and is shown in Loggan's

Detail from Loggan's 17th Century
engraving of Christ's College,
Cambridge

engravings of the time which also depict two others standing in college
gardens.

London's Dovehouse Street in Chelsea marks the approximate site of a
dovecote which must have existed in very early times when the district was
still completely rural. An engraved map dated 1699 shows that the kitchen
garden of Beaufort House, near present-day Beaufort Street, was called
Dovecote Close, but no building is marked. The original dovecote may
have been attached either to Sir Thomas More's earlier manor house on
that site or possibly to Henry VIII's Chelsea Palace which was nearby in
Cheyne Walk.

## Rights to Build

The Normans brought with them the feudal right to own a dovecote and
although it has often been said that this privilege was protected by law,
there does not seem to have been any legal basis for it. At that time the rule
of 'might is right' largely prevailed and over the years this became
consolidated through usage into what is legally termed 'use and wont'.
Originally the barons enjoyed the dovecote privilege, but it was soon
shared by the church, that other great power in the land, and later also by

lords of the manor. There was little conflict in those early days, because in economic and practical terms building a dovecote was quite out of reach of the poor. So the custom became firmly entrenched and was seldom challenged.

From the 14th century onwards, partly as a consequence of the Black Death, slow but important changes took place in many aspects of the feudal system. Several precedents were established when some lords of the manor allowed a few of the new class of yeoman tenant farmers to build their own dovecotes. As a result of this and following the Dissolution of the monasteries, restrictions on building them had weakened considerably towards the end of the 16th century. However, the legal position appears to have remained ambiguous and in 1577 a tenant was ordered by the court to demolish a dovecote that he had erected on the estate of a royal manor.

By the early 17th century Gervaise Markham, in his work *The English Husbandman*, was able to say that common sense had begun to rule the day and that the right to build a dovecote was being extended at last. However, it does not seem to have been a general freedom and tenants still could not build without the landowner's licence. This point is made a century later in the *New Law Dictionary* of 1750 which states that 'a person may have a pigeon house or dovecote by prescription'. In practice, however, large numbers of dovecotes were built from Elizabethan times onwards by the new class of prosperous freeholders and tenant farmers. A natural reaction to this sharing of an ancient privilege was that dovecotes often became regarded as status symbols.

The loss of grain due to the voracious pigeons feeding on land outside the owner's boundaries increased as the numbers of dovecotes multiplied; there were said to be 26,000 in England in the mid-17th century, but the accuracy of this much quoted statistic cannot be assessed. It seems to have been a persistent problem, because as late as 1797 a certain John Selden dogmatically aired his views thus:

> *Some men make it a case of conscience whether a man may have a pidgeon house, because his pidgeons eat other folk's corn. But there is no such thing as conscience in the business: the matter is whether he be a man of such quality that the state allows him to have a dove house: if so there's an end of the business, his pidgeons have a right to eat where they please themselves.*

It has been estimated that 500 pairs of pigeons could eat 13,000 bushels of corn annually. This theoretical calculation is not well supported by evidence and was based solely on the contents of the birds' crops at harvest time; it takes no account of their completely different diet at other times of the year. However, serious objections to the birds' depredations were still being raised during the 19th century at which time a tax on dovecotes was proposed, but the popularity of the dovecote was already in marked decline and so the idea of any legislation was dropped. An approach to the same problem in France after the Revolution compelled owners to confine their birds to the dovecotes during sowing and harvest times.

The grudge felt by the rural population against the pigeons and their owners was much exacerbated by their being forbidden to molest or destroy the birds, whatever damage they caused. However ambiguous the law in relation to dovecote ownership, its position concerning those caught stealing or killing the birds was unequivocal. As early as the 12th century there is mention of 'those who take pigeons by nets or other Engines to the Destruction of Pigeon Houses' and a law of the 14th century laid the foundations for the punishment of poachers. The penalties were severe, three months in prison for the first and second offences and up until 1579 the death penalty was possible for the third. In the age of firearms, later legislation gave added protection to the pigeon in an 18th century Act which forbade shooting within 600 paces of a hennery and 100 paces of a pigeon house. Not until very much later was the right of an owner upheld by a Court of the Queen's Bench to shoot a pigeon on his own crops.

It is possible that the damage done to crops by dovecote pigeons in the past has been exaggerated; it has certainly never been satisfactorily substantiated. Recent observation has shown that the birds are well adapted to a varied diet, consuming quantities of weed seeds in addition to grain and this has been claimed as a benefit to farmers. Real damage to crops could only have been inflicted by very large numbers of birds when the seed was newly sown; this is confirmed by the old saying 'Sow four grains in a row; one for the pigeon, one for the crow; one to rot and one to grow'. They do not and cannot eat the standing corn and following the harvest they merely devour spilled grain in the stubble; surely a harmless enough pursuit? Gilbert White believed that wood pigeons were much more destructive. Present-day reports of large flocks of these birds descending on the fields of East Anglia from Scandinavia seem to confirm his view.

*CHAPTER VI*

# Later Circular Dovecotes

The early circular base-plan continued to be used over the centuries even after new shapes and styles had been introduced. As late as the 17th century the great French writer on husbandry, Olivier de Serres, stressed its advantages and an authority of the 18th century, quoted in the *English Sportsman's Dictionary*, echoed his view. Their preference was based partly on the fact that this pattern was best adapted for the installation of that useful interior device, known as a potence, by means of which squabs and eggs could be easily collected at all levels and partly on the dubious supposition that the curved exterior walls would deter cats, rats, weasels and other creatures from getting inside.

Circular dovecotes from medieval times onwards are still to be found scattered about the country. Exact dating is seldom possible on con-structional grounds alone because the same building techniques and materials were often employed over several centuries. Inscribed dates which are sometimes found may refer primarily to rebuilding or restora-tion work and are not always helpful. Occasionally, mortar comparison with other nearby buildings of known date may provide a positive clue to age.

One important factor influencing the survival of several ancient examples in the south-west is the availability and early use of local stone. Conversely, the complete disappearance of the most primitive dovecote of all, which was built of mud, clay or cob (clay bound with chopped straw) for the walls and thatch for the roof, is due to the impermanence of these materials. However, some mud remains have recently been reported in Nottinghamshire. The notable shortage of building stone, apart from flint, in East Anglia explains the absence of circular stone dovecotes and favours the use of brick in that part of the country. Essex, for example, has only one circular dovecote still standing; it is brick-built and of relatively late date. In Hertfordshire there are no surviving circular examples whatever.

In many counties the use of different building materials according to period and locality has produced a great variety of circular dovecotes, even within a single district. Limestone and sandstone of all types and colour, flint, chalk clunch and occasionally granite and slate have all been used. Towards the end of the 17th century brick became widely available for humble domestic dwellings and farm buildings and later ousted local stone, mainly for economic reasons. In addition to these different building

materials, local traditions and standards of construction varied widely in the past, so that although the base-plan may be the same, no two dovecotes are identical in every detail. This is an attractive and intriguing feature which dovecotes share with other early examples of vernacular architecture.

## Exterior Characteristics

Many of the features to be described in relation to the circular dovecote are just as applicable to the square, rectangular and even the later octagonal designs which will be considered later.

The very earliest dovecotes have massive rubblestone, windowless walls which often measure between three and four feet in thickness. It is generally believed that the thicker the walls, the older the building and most ancient examples seem to follow this rule, which may be helpful in any assessment. However, in spite of their mass, patchy repairs and ominous bulges are evident in the walls of many surviving cotes, although the support of external buttresses appears to have largely controlled the problem in others. In Cornwall a few dovecotes of rare dry-stone construction have survived with the help of more recent cement pointing. Post-medieval walls were less massive and often built of roughly coursed stone; even later, elegant ashlar stone construction was introduced.

An interesting variation of the stone rotunda is characteristic of the northern counties and Scotland and many are still to be found. These dovecotes are sometimes described as 'tun-bellied' —a tun being a large

Tun-bellied dovecote at Aberdour, Fifeshire

84

wine cask — and are believed to date from the 16th century. They differ from their southern counterparts in that their walls bulge outwards and then taper upwards. Their roof is a shallow dome and they generally consist of three or four stages each marked externally by a raised band of masonry or cincture. These string courses, sometimes known as rat courses, often encompass dovecote walls of all types at various levels. Unlike their use in other buildings, they were not necessarily decorative, but were designed as obstacles to climbing animal intruders, but if level and sufficiently wide, they also served as perching ledges for the birds.

In early dovecotes, doorways are characteristically small and low, often less than four feet high, so that an adult has to bend double to get inside.

Doorways:
*(top left)* Nash's Farm, Comberton;
*(top right)* Kinwarton;
and with *voussoirs* at
*(bottom left)* Hyde's House, Dinton
*(bottom right)* Hurley

An extreme example at Bussow in Cornwall is only 27 inches in height. It is believed that they were deliberately built in this way to prevent the exit of thieves bearing nets or hampers full of birds, but it may otherwise have been to reduce the silhouette of anyone entering, an event which inevitably causes much disturbance and 'fluttering in the dovecote'. Considerations of security definitely account for one of the most unusual dovecotes of all in Cornwall, which unfortunately is no longer in existence. Described as being like a well above ground, it had no door at all and access must have been a laborious matter: 'You could not get in or out but by fetching a ladder, when you got atop the wall you pulled up the ladder and dropped it down inside. So you see 'twas built so it wasn't easy to rob the culverhouse'. Many doorways consist of crude, square openings with roughly shaped stone or wooden lintels and jambs, but in a few dovecotes they are more elaborately constructed and have arched, lancet or segmental heads. Occasionally, later doorways were finely executed in ashlar stone; in some cases existing apertures were enlarged and dressed importantly. As for the doors themselves, most of them being made of wood have perished and been replaced over the years. However, there are a few survivors constructed of solid oak and fixed with wrought-iron nails. The ever-present preoccupation with security would have required some form of locking and also explains the occasional use of double doors, sometimes made of metal.

Only a few of the original domed, corbelled, stone roofs have survived, but at Allington Castle in Kent and Holcombe Rogus in Devon a tiled roof is superimposed upon the earlier inner stone vaulting. Later roofs are mainly conical in form and are made of thatch, stone tiles or slate. Elegant variations are to be found in the use of graded tiles of fissile limestone or sandstone, bearing local names such as Collyweston, Stonesfield and Horsham 'slates'. Some roofs were designed with deep overhanging eaves as an additional precaution against intruders. Rarely, a two-gabled roof, possibly a reconstruction, caps a circular dovecote with odd effect as at see page 90 Little Badminton in Gloucestershire. Equally unusual is the magnificent see page 90 ogival slate roof with matching cupola at Halswell House in North Somerset, which was destroyed by fire in the Second World War and subsequently restored by the US Army.

Several other alterations and additions to the design of dovecotes were introduced over the centuries. An *oculus* in the roof open to the sky may have suited Roman dovecotes in the Mediterranean, but it brought problems when copied in wet northern climes. Pigeons are more prone to disease in damp conditions and in addition the accumulated droppings on the floor become more difficult to manage. Another complication arose with the installation of wooden potences which were subject to rot. The addition of a cupola, also known as a glover or lantern, above the summit opening, to protect the interior from rain, but which also allows the birds

Norton-sub-Hamdon. Originally attached to the manor house, it became enclosed when the churchyard was extended.

see page 91
see page 91

to come and go, was therefore an early necessity and has become a familiar feature. Early designs were simple and generally executed in stone, but later they became more ornamental and were often surmounted by a weathervane or pole and ball. Such versions were usually made of wood, sometimes faced with lead and glazed in part, but being delicate and in an exposed position, many have been replaced, often with imaginative and unusual modern designs. Some wooden cupolas are panelled and fretted with entry holes and perching ledges for the birds as at Athelhampton in Dorset and Rougham Hall in Norfolk.

In old dovecotes little light reached the interior through the summit opening even on a sunny summer's day and the installation of any sort of cupola must have made conditions murkier. Dormer windows and openings in the main walls were probably intended as a remedy but also served as additional flight-holes for the birds and may sometimes have been added as an afterthought. Good dormers are to be seen at Richards Castle in Herefordshire and Norton-sub-Hamdon in Somerset, also at Rousham in Oxfordshire. The fitting of external shutters may have been intended to exclude marauders at night or to trap the birds inside the dovecote during periodical culling. In a few dovecotes, and invariably in those without cupola or window openings for the birds, large single portals or several rows of flight-holes with alighting ledges are placed high up in the walls or gables.

Projecting iron spikes below or between entrance holes, few of which have been preserved, prevented netting being secured by thieves. This ruse was prevalent at the time when large numbers of birds were stolen for pigeon-shooting matches.

## Building Materials

When available locally, stone continued to be much used for building. In later dovecotes, roughly coursed blocks of limestone or sandstone replaced the earlier rubblestone walls, while in the 18th century, ashlar stone gave an elegant finish as at Farmington Lodge in Gloucestershire and the unusual Ham Hill stone cote at Compton House in Dorset. Striking colour variations give additional interest to this group. For example, the pale limestone at Minster Lovell in Oxfordshire, the cold grey of blue lias at Shapwick Manor in Somerset, the dark ochre of marlstone at Melplash Court in Dorset, the red sandstone of Holm Lacy in Worcestershire and the grey and pink hues of Sarsen sandstone at Avebury Manor in Wiltshire are just a few illustrations. Occasionally, the walls are decorated with horizontal bands of knapped flint as at Athelhampton in Dorset. Flint, when it occurs naturally has been a substitute for stone in several counties and was sometimes a component of rubblestone construction early on, but later was used on its own, either plain or knapped, sometimes coursed and also contrasted with brick. Sussex, being particularly rich in flint buildings of all kinds, possesses three excellent early circular, flint dovecotes, probably dating from the 16th or 17th centuries. At Patcham and Motcombe Farm the thick walls are constructed entirely of plain flint, while at Hangleton Manor a total reconstruction which includes coursed flint walls and chalk nesting places has now been completed.

see page 91

The introduction of brick in the 17th century, used either alone or in combination with other materials, contributed a great deal to the charm and variety of later dovecotes. Many plain, unadorned, red brick circular cotes have been preserved in excellent condition. At Broughton in Hampshire, the well-restored dovecote stands amongst the headstones in the churchyard. At Whitton Hall in a remote part of Shropshire, the dovecote stands picturesquely at one end of a beautiful walled garden. By contrast, in well-to-do Surrey suburbia, a dovecote is to be found in a corner of the grounds of the exclusive Royal Automobile Club near Epsom.

One of the most attractive combinations of materials to be found is brick and flint. In Oxfordshire, a striking effect at Ipsden Manor comprises vertical alternating bands, while at Wilcot Manor in Wiltshire they run horizontally. Brick was also successfully contrasted with stone. At Ockwells Manor in Berkshire a red brick dovecote has four full-height, stepped, stone buttresses. Conversely, at Parham Park in Sussex, the four large bull's-eye apertures high up on the walls, together with the arched doorway are outlined in brick which contrasts well with the pale sandstone structure.

It is important not to overlook the concept of 'façadism' in which

88

A variety of building materials. Stone at Embleton - primitive appearance, but 17th century; flint and brick at Ipsden; rubblestone at The Manor, Wellow; green sandstone at Parham; brick with stone dressings at Ockwells Manor, Cox Green; flint at Patcham

89

Contrasting roofs at Little Badminton, Halswell House and Rothersthorpe

90

Group of circular dovecotes: *(top left)* Athelhampton; *(top right)* Court Lodge Farm, Horton Kirby; *(bottom left)* Court House, Richards Castle; *(bottom right)* Rousham Park

Picturesque dovecote at Walcot Hall, Lydbury

92

Adapted fortified manor tower at Faulstone House, Bishopstone

*(top)* Dovecote as landscape ornament at Witton Castle
*(bottom)* Large tower dovecote within kitchen garden at Coleshill

*(top)* Sulham 'folly' dovecote
*(bottom)* Neglected Gothic Revival tower at Davenport House

Unusual variant at Upper Harlestone built of ironstone with Collyweston tiles, probably 15th century

updating of a building was achieved by cladding. At Sufton in Herefordshire, the original circular stone dovecote has been totally transformed by a later brick skin; the two superimposed layers can now be clearly seen because the building is in a ruinous state and the walls are falling down.

In all this, whatever the materials used, variation in size plays an important part. At Madresfield Court in Worcestershire, the exceptionally large brick edifice, which strictly qualifies as a tower, dominates the surrounding Victorian farmyard, while the small but charming one at Holbrook House in Somerset is tucked away beside the stables and is less than half the size.

## Towers

Dovecotes in the form of towers having a circular base-plan, probably date from very early times, as they are simply an upward extension of the fundamental plan. Palladius, the 4th century Roman writer on husbandry, whose works were translated into English in the 15th century, makes reference to a pigeon tower as 'a toure with plaine and whited walls and fenestelles IIII, a columbaire'. This suggests that the Romans built this type of dovecote in addition to those of beehive and tortoise shape. A manuscript illustration shows that the French had adopted this form of construction by the 15th century. Unfortunately, very few of these spectacular buildings still exist.

In this country, the earliest and largest stands beside the church at Sibthorpe in Nottinghamshire. It was built in 1325 on a grange belonging

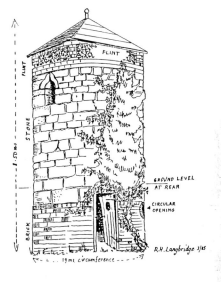

*(left)* Madresfield (see also p.201)
*(right)* Sibthorpe

97

Westenhanger, past and present

see page 93

to Sibthorpe Abbey; it is 50 feet high and forms a landmark for miles around. Pevsner describes it as being most impressive in its isolation and simplicity. It has slightly battered rubblestone walls, a new conical roof and contains more than 1,000 nest-holes. A tower of quite different character is to be found at Bishopstone in Wiltshire, where it forms a conspicuous feature on the front lawn of Faulstone House. It has pronounced horizontal flint and stone banding on one aspect and some interesting flushwork decoration above the door. This tower is the sole remnant of the original 14th century fortified manor, but although known to have been used as a dovecote for well over a century it is suspected that this was a subsequent adaptation. The interior is now divided into two stages, the upper one of which has been fitted, unusually, with an upstairs potence. At Westenhanger in Kent, fragments remain of a large 14th century house which is believed to have once been a royal manor, also fortified. Originally it was a quadrangular building, but the only part to have survived intact is one of its circular corner towers, which is now a well-preserved dovecote. It is not known whether accommodation for the birds was provided when the manor was built or whether, like Faulstone House, it was adapted later. The dovecote now stands picturesquely against the much later Queen Anne house from which access to the interior is gained via the first floor landing.

98

Springhill, County Londonderry

In Northern Ireland, a slender whitewashed pigeon tower with a conical roof abuts one end of a range of stableyard buildings at Springhill in County Londonderry. The 17th century 'Planter' house was built for a family which arrived from Ayrshire and the dovecote dates from the same time. Two narrow slits in the upper walls provide access for the birds and it contains nesting niches from top to bottom, although additional floors have been inserted.

The mansion of Coleshill in Oxfordshire, that elegant example of early classical architecture designed by Roger Pratt in 1650, was destroyed by fire in 1952 and subsequently pulled down. The handsome plain stone tower dovecote in the grounds is believed to be coeval with the house. It abuts one wall of the large, neglected kitchen garden and is under the care of the National Trust. see page 94

A much later 18th century brick tower dovecote stands in the centre of the stable-yard of Kennel Farm at Amersham in Buckinghamshire. This massive, stark tower, locally often referred to as a silo, has been squatly re-roofed and the whitewashed walls barely conceal patterns of vitrified headers in the brickwork. The impressive, spacious interior contains over 1,000 nesting places built to a high standard of workmanship. It must have been intended to serve a large household, probably the nearby 18th century mansion, Shardeloes, designed by Stiff Leadbetter and Robert Adam.

## Landscape Ornaments

see page 94

see page 95

see page 95

Several towers of attractive design fall into the category of landscape ornaments. At Witton Castle in County Durham the pretty three-stage, battlemented dovecote stands prominently on a grassy hill. It is built of coursed ashlar sandstone and houses pigeons in the two upper storeys. The ground floor, with gothic arcades, provides a summerhouse or belvedere. A brick, two-storeyed tower also in neo-Gothic style, probably dating from the early 19th century, stands in isolation on a knoll at Sulham in Berkshire in full view of the M4 motorway, close to exit 12. Locally it is regarded as a folly and the exterior much resembles one. Unfortunately, the roof has collapsed and some battlements are missing, but pigeons can be seen to be still occupying nest-holes inside the top storey. The ground floor, with its three lanceolate arched entrances and domed ceiling, affords splendid views of the surrounding countryside and may also have been intended as a belvedere. At Davenport in Shropshire a brick-built tower in Gothic Revival style contains nesting places from top to bottom, but is in a very decrepit state. It has a pretty corbel table at roof springer level and is decorated with a number of arrow slits.

*CHAPTER VII*

# Square and Rectangular Designs

Although most of the oldest surviving dovecotes are circular in plan a few ancient square and rectangular varieties are also still standing. Very many others have disappeared without trace because, like most domestic and farm buildings of Norman and medieval times they were timber-built. This pattern, once introduced, continued to be used over the centuries until eventually square dovecotes outnumbered all other varieties put together. They now comprise a very large group indeed and although many in it are plain and unpretentious, several unusual and attractive variations such as the picturesque black-and-white examples and the four-gabled design chiefly to be found in the Cotswolds, are included. In addition, the use of different building materials and varying local traditions have combined to make square dovecotes follow the general rule that no two are identical in every detail.

**External Features**

Certain broad characteristics can be identified in the group as a whole. Roofs take several forms; double-pitched with two, four, or rarely, six gables; hipped (pyramidal) or half-hipped, both occasionally including miniature gables or gablets. The mono-pitched variety, so commonly found in French and Scottish dovecotes, was not used in England. Cupolas on summits still exist in great variety, although many have been removed and the roof opening capped. As well as protecting the interior from rain they served to admit light, air and/or the birds and their structure was adapted accordingly. Early examples are rugged and simple and include a few in which the cupola echoes the design of the dovecote itself, as in the pyramidal effect at Wytham in Oxfordshire and the four-gabled version at Luntley Court, Herefordshire. Some of the unusual cruciform variants of lantern were prettily decorated. Writing in the 1920s, Donald Smith described some Essex cotes with elaborate gablet bargeboards and another in which a central classical arched opening was used.

Dormer windows are not found in four-gabled dovecotes and seldom exist in square dovecotes with other types of roof. Where they do occur, as recorded on an engraving of the much altered dovecote at Berwick in

see page 116

Dovecote at 'White Hart', Wytham

Sussex and also at present-day Long Crendon, Buckinghamshire, and Abbotsbury, Dorset, they are only minor features.

Single openings in walls or gables, sometimes of the *oeil de boeuf* variety, or square, provide additional or alternative entrances for the birds and occasionally a row of holes below the eaves serves the same purpose.

One or more string courses, or rat courses, often encircle the outside walls and, as in round cotes, may be used by the birds as perching ledges. In addition to such barriers, projecting metal plates affixed to the angles of walls several feet up have been described; sharp spikes sticking out of the ground immediately below were optimistically intended to impale the falling victims. Two dovecotes in Herefordshire were reported to be equipped in this way a century or so ago. A more radical precaution against climbing animal marauders was to raise the whole dovecote on piers, as at Penpont in Powys. However, this method seems to have been seldom employed although it was standard practice in granaries, using staddle-stones, and a common feature of French dovecotes, in which it served a totally different purpose in some regions. The so-called *colombier-sur-piliers* was designed to evade the legal restrictions attached to ownership of a dovecote having substantial foundations in the ground, the *colombier-à-pied*.

The thoughtful provision of multiple sunning ledges is a feature peculiar to square dovecotes but very few are to be found. An excellent example, however, at Staunton Grange, Nottinghamshire, consists of six full-length brick ledges on each of three walls.

102

Frocester Court

Doorways tend to follow the general rule that the older the dovecote the smaller their size, while the thickness of walls is also considered to be indicative of their age. The later brick-built dovecotes have much thinner walls than their predecessors and often appear to be constructed of two skins, the inner being the nest-bearing layer. This contrasts with most ancient stone walls whose nests were built within their total thickness.

## Earliest Square and Rectangular Designs

Early documentation seldom specifies the precise shape of a dovecote, but there are a few exceptions. A graphic description dated 1567 records details of one at the site of an early monastery of the Carmelite Friars at Hulne Priory in Northumberland, '...right over on the other side of the way is a lyttle dove-kette four squared covered with sklaite now repaired by his lordship wherein is a good flight of doves'.

Most of the earliest square and oblong dovecotes that remain belonged to religious establishments and although their design is generally unremarkable, a few have interesting features and two are of particular archaeological interest. Recent excavations on the site of the medieval Benedictine estate at Frocester Court, Gloucestershire, have included a study of the double, rectangular, monastic pigeon house of which about half the original still stands. Analysis of the mortar has established that it is coeval with the adjacent 13th century tithe barn. The exceptional point of interest is in the central nest-bearing partition which incorporates re-used

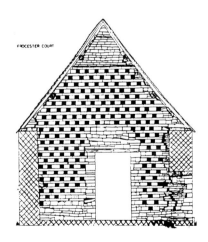

103

fragments of 11th century columns and capitals whose source is believed to have been the Norman parish church which was rebuilt in the early 13th century. A similar discovery was made at another double rectangular dovecote at the Manor House, Hayling Island, Hampshire, which is built on the site of a moated grange belonging to the nearby, but long-since vanished Benedictine priory on the coast. This was destroyed by an inundation from the sea in 1325 at which time it is believed that the monks retreated to the grange and used pieces of Caen stone from the ruins to enlarge and rebuild the dovecote. Several pieces of worked stone, including fragments of a Norman arch are to be seen in the inside walls. Crude stone nesting places are fitted in the main walls, but a much later partition constructed of small pre-Reformation bricks carries nesting places on both sides. Deeply grooved claw marks on the threshold of these nest-hole openings, due to the shortage of alighting ledges, are vivid reminders of the birds' centuries of occupation. The exteriors of both these oblong dovecotes are quite plain and nowadays could easily be taken for any farm or garden outbuilding. The same is not true of the early square stone pigeon house which originally belonged to the Augustinian

see page 114

canons of Notley Abbey, Buckinghamshire, founded in the 12th century. Standing in splendid isolation in an open field, it is situated above and at a short distance from the 15th century abbot's lodging. It has been dated variously, but was probably built in the 16th century with stone fragments from the abbey, several moulded pieces of which have been found in the core of the walls. It is an outstanding example of its type and has recently been well restored. The unusual interior contains more than 1,000 nests due to the ingenious addition of four nest-bearing piers which project from the middle of each inner wall.

Another large monastic dovecote stands in a meadow beside the well-known 15th century tithe barn at Abbotsbury in Dorset. It is a stone, double-chambered oblong building with two unusual metal cupolas and two small dormers and is believed to be of the same date as the barn. These two buildings and the swannery are all that remain of the Benedictine abbey founded in the 11th century. A few miles away at Puncknowle, on the possible site of a monastic grange farm belonging to the abbey, there is a small rectangular stone dovecote which has been ascribed to the 13th century. Recent meticulous restorative work has included replacement of the roof with graded Purbeck stone tiles. Other notable details are the 'medieval stitching' using thin stone slivers to bind an upper corner of the outer walls and an inner wooden doorway of cruck construction. The inner walls of stone and chalk clunch present a striking appearance having vertical lines of crude square nest-hole openings.

Members of the strict order of Carthusian monks lived in seclusion and silence for most of the time, but several material advantages compensated for the rigours of their existence. In some establishments, each monk was

Early monastic dovecotes at
Hayling Island *(top)* and Abbotsbury

105

Witham Friary

provided with a small house set in a walled garden containing a privy and he was allowed to keep a dog and a dovecote. At Mount Grace Charterhouse in Yorkshire there are remains of the priory and the monks' dwellings, but not surprisingly there is no trace of any individual dovecotes. There are, however, substantial remains of large communal dovecotes at some of their other houses. At Witham Friary, Somerset, where parts of the first English Carthusian monastery are incorporated into the parish church, there is an oblong, rubblestone dovecote, a survival from the monastic estate. Unfortunately, there are few, if any, remaining signs of its original function, apart from some nest-holes in one inside wall. It has been converted into a village amenity and the mullioned windows may date from that time. At Hinton Charterhouse in Avon, remains of the 13th century priory include a three-storeyed, four-gabled building which comprises a vaulted chapel on the ground floor and an elegant room called a library on the middle floor, next to which is a self-contained dovecote. A spiral staircase leads into another integral dovecote in the top storey, whose two lancet gable openings provided access for the birds. At Norton St Philip, fairly close by, there is an oblong stone cote with Tudor details on a site believed to have been a grange belonging to Hinton Priory.

106

Hinton Charterhouse

DOVE COTE & CHURCH ———— PENMON-

On Anglesey a large rubblestone, square dovecote stands close to the ruined 12th century Benedictine Penmon Priory of which only parts of the church and refectory remain. The dovecote has an unusual four-sided domed stone roof with interior corbel construction. An interesting feature is the interior central stone column which reaches a considerable height and has projecting stone steps set spirally. The dovecote is said to date from the 16th century, but may well be earlier.

In addition to these early ecclesiastical dovecotes there are a few surviving secular examples generally attached to medieval manors. At Brompton Low Hall in North Yorkshire, a rectangular pigeon house built of rough limestone blocks set in clay and having a low, arched doorway, is all that remains of the 15th century manor house. An early square rubblestone dovecote on a smaller scale, and probably manorial in origin, is situated at Luckington Court, Wiltshire. Its exterior, which resembles a small chapel, is quite plain apart from two ball finials at each end of the roof ridge and one slit opening above the door for the birds. It contains about 500 nests which, like many other early examples, are roughly widened at the back without a pronounced left or right turn. The present Queen Anne house replaced a much earlier Elizabethan building for which the dovecote was probably built.

## Outsize Buildings

Some of the early rectangular dovecotes were very large indeed, but the biggest of all at St Pancras Priory, Lewes, in Sussex, was unfortunately demolished in about 1800. Engravings show that it resembled a parish

*Ancient Dove-cote at Lewes Priory*

*(top)* Large, crow-stepped gabled, double dovecote at Willington
*(bottom)* Culham Manor dovecote

church in shape and size. It is said to have contained 3,328 nesting cells of hewn chalk which means that it could accommodate a very large number of adult birds. Its only surviving rival, and one which now has a good claim to being the largest in England is at Culham Manor in Oxfordshire. This stone double dovecote carries the date 1685 above the door. It now has a red tiled roof, probably a replacement, and contains more than 3,000 brick niches which line all available surfaces of the walls, gables, and the dividing partition. The interior presents an altogether overpowering impression. Several other oblong dovecotes which were built on the grand scale are still standing. At Newton-in-the-Willows, Northamptonshire, the 16th century dovecote, which is all that remains of the manor house belonging to the Treshams, stands in grand isolation with only the parish church of the

Newton-in-the-Willows dovecote and parish church

vanished village in view a field away. It is an austere-looking, stone-built, double-chambered building with two cupolas and a low, arched entrance door to each half, containing over 2,000 nests in total. A dovecote of similar type and size at Ashby St Ledgers, also in Northamptonshire, is one of two standing in the grounds of the hall.

## French Lecterns and Dutch Gables

Among these outsize rectangular dovecotes, the most notable of all is at Willington in Bedfordshire. This spectacular double-chambered building, decorated with crow-stepped gables, contains more than 1,300 nests and was built in 1530 by Sir John Goswick, Cardinal Wolsey's Master of Horse. Its interest lies not only in its size, but in the design of its roof which gives it a resemblance to the lean-to, so-called 'lectern' type of dovecote. Although

111

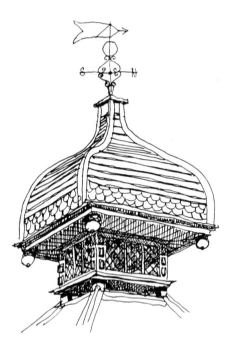

see page 117

this form of construction is common in Scotland and in parts of the south of France, there do not appear to be others like it in England. The general concept seems to have been to protect pigeons from the prevailing wind. The true lectern dovecote has a mono-pitched roof which is sometimes fitted with high parapet walls to give additional shelter. Access for the birds is provided either by dormers or, less commonly, by a full-width louvred 'clerestory' opening halfway up the roof. At Willington this leads into a spacious interior long gallery for the birds, from which they can enter the main chambers.

The use of stepped gables was a Dutch or Flemish influence introduced in the 17th century and was extensively used in Scotland, but less commonly in the south. Examples known to be embellished in this way are two rugged, square stone dovecotes at Faenol Fawr, Bodelwyddan, and Gop Farm, Trelawnyd, both in Clwyd, and the larger oblong limestone pigeon house at Brompton in Yorkshire.

Apart from the crow-stepped decoration, Dutch or Flemish gables are a feature of several square and rectangular brick dovecotes, two of which are of impressive size and design. A large 19th century version at Wolverley, Worcestershire, has four Dutch gables, each having central circular openings which were probably the original flight-holes, but are now blocked off. This edifice stood derelict for some time, but has now been converted into an unusual three-storeyed house. At Hawley Manor in Kent, one of the Dutch-style gable ends of the three dormer windows carries the date 1556, but there is some doubt as to its authenticity. The dovecote's most prominent feature, however, is the uncommonly large ogival cupola suggesting a more oriental than Dutch influence. Two less imposing dovecotes also incorporate this type of gable. At Goswold Hall in Suffolk, a rectangular structure, unfortunately in poor repair, has Dutch gabled ends, while at Tytherington in Wiltshire a modest three-storey building has an arched gable carrying a row of flight-holes which give access to what was once the upper pigeon loft.

**Later Stone Buildings**

Square and rectangular dovecotes continued to be built from medieval times onwards in most parts of the country. Before the use of brick had become widespread towards the end of the 17th century, local stone continued to be used in building construction. Existing examples include many which are plain and unassuming as at Caddenham Manor, Corsham Court, Easton House, all in Wiltshire, and Mappercombe, Dorset, while variations in building material give heightened interest as, for example, the use of chalk ashlar at Bessingby in Yorkshire. Architectural features such as the four-centred, arched wall-openings at Norton St Philip, Avon,

112

Ogival cupola at Hawley Manor

113

Large dovecote near Notley Abbey at Long Crendon

Snowshill

115

Dovecote raised on piers at Penpont

116

Upper loft at Tytherington

*(top left)* Millichope Park; *(top right)* Brightwell Park;
*(bottom left)* Pigeon Tower at Bruton; *(bottom right)* Six-gabled double dovecote at Lower Slaughter

118

*(top left)* Temple Thornton; *(top right)* flint pigeon loft at Edburton;
*(bottom)* Classical four-gabled Cotswold dovecote at Fiddington Manor

Elaborate four-gabled example with cruciform gablets to match, at Godminster

and Arreton Manor on the Isle of Wight, may be helpful in dating. Others are notable for their attractive situation, either in lovely gardens, as at Lee Farm, Sussex, or linked with a range of handsome buildings like those at Cosgrove Hall, Northamptonshire. There is also a small number of idiosyncratic square dovecotes which do not fit easily into any particular category, as at Millichope, Shropshire, where the dovecote resembles a non-conformist chapel and at Brightwell Park, Oxfordshire, where the base-plan is in the form of a Greek cross. In addition there is the rare example at Hinton-on-the-Green, Worcestershire, where two oblong see page 118
see page 118

*(top)* Lee Farm, Fittleworth
*(bottom)* Cosgrove Hall

121

dovecotes are built above and on either side of a large connecting archway.

There are several square stone dovecotes of relatively late date which consist of more than one storey, generally two, but occasionally three, the birds occupying the top floor. Some are purely practical structures which stand alone in the farmyard or form part of a continuous range of see page 115 outbuildings. Others are sited in gardens, as at Snowshill Manor, Gloucestershire, where an exterior stone staircase leads to the upper pigeon house. Two more elaborate cotes of later date at Hermitage Farm, Burghill and Bollitree Castle, both in Herefordshire, are said to be French in style and once contained nests in the upper storeys. Their present see page 119 glazed cupolas are almost certainly replacements. At Temple Thornton in Northumberland the sombre grey stone edifice is said have been modelled on the local parish church tower and is of a quite different character.

A photograph taken early this century at Baginton, Warwickshire, records another variation of a two-storeyed dovecote, which unfortunately no longer exists. It shows an attractive square building with a hipped roof, windows and a chimney. This was a combined dovecote and summerhouse and is characteristic of what was often called a banqueting house in the 17th century. At that time, the dessert or final course of a formal dinner was known as the banquet and in summer was often enjoyed out-of-doors in one of these little houses, some of which were grander than others. Similar buildings in ornamental style, variously known as pleasure houses, tea rooms, garden pavilions or, if the views were good, gazebos, belvederes and prospect towers, were built in the 18th century as a reflection of the developing English taste for enjoying the pleasures of gardens and grounds. They were often sited at points of vantage and were sometimes fitted up for use as an occasional sleeping place as well as recreation during the day. Accommodation for pigeons was sometimes provided in the top storey. Another good example is the three-storeyed garden pavilion at Bishop Oak, County Durham.

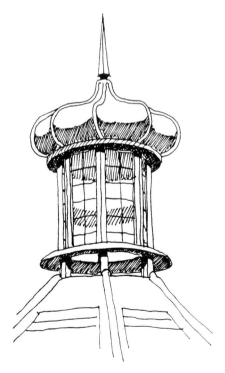

## Square Towers

A few of the dovecotes with more than one floor are tall enough to qualify as towers, but in most cases the pigeons occupied only a small part of the space. The need to keep large numbers of birds was already in marked decline when they were built. None of these buildings can compare with the vast early circular towers which were built solely to house enormous flocks of birds. One of the earliest three-storeyed towers formerly existing at St Buryan, in Cornwall, is believed to have been built in about 1500. It occupied the corner of a two acre, walled rabbit warren which was entered through its ground floor. The top storey, reached by ladder from outside, housed the pigeons and the middle floor became a garden or prospect room.

122

Baginton dovecote in 1900; no longer standing

see page 118

see page 119

The origin of the so-called pigeon tower at Bruton in Somerset poses something of a mystery. The tall, roofless ruin stands on a hill and is a local landmark. What remains is the shell of a three-storeyed building with mullioned windows in the two lower stages, but all the floors have gone. Today, rows of pigeon-holes in the upper part are visible from the interior. The local people believe that the dovecote once housed the pigeons of the vanished Augustinian priory, but the small number of holes and the style of building are uncharacteristic of such an early date. An equally untenable theory is that it is a converted watchtower. The more probable explanation is that it was built as a prospect tower and an engraving showing a chimney and the remains of a fireplace on one floor supports this view. The adjacent former priory was owned by the Berkeleys before being demolished in 1780 and they may have built the tower during their occupation.

A well-preserved, heavily-buttressed, stone two-storey tower at Abington Park, Northamptonshire, is dated 1678. It once housed a well and water-wheel on the ground floor and the birds still occupy the floor above. At Edburton Farm, Sussex, a slender flint-built example adjoins the outbuildings and contains a small pigeon loft at the top, reached by ladder from inside. The well-known Pigeon Tower at Rivington in Lancashire was built in 1910 for William Lever in the grounds of his home. The two lower floors housed pigeons and the top floor was a comfortable room from which wide views could be enjoyed.

**Four Gables**

see page 119

Four-gabled stone dovecotes are characteristic of the Cotswold tradition and many are still standing in Gloucestershire, as at Naunton, Coln St Aldwyns, Weston-sub-Edge and Fiddington, but a few are to be found in other districts, generally just beyond its borders. A plain, square design of one storey is most common, but rectangular and two- or three- floored varieties add interest to the group. Most of the Gloucestershire dovecotes are built of local limestone and many still have their original Stonesfield stone roofs, often with graded tiles. Their cupolas are also sometimes four-gabled to match.

One of the earliest stone dovecotes of this pattern to have survived was originally attached to the medieval manor at Westington, Chipping Campden, Gloucestershire, and is believed to be the one mentioned in Worcester Cathedral Rolls of 1295. It stands today in an excellent state of repair and possesses the unusual feature of four partial rat courses clasping each angle of the outside walls, about six feet from the ground. A decorative sundial, a later addition in 1679, is placed above the entrance door which faces the house. The interior is fitted with a potence,

124

Cotswold dovecote, Naunton

uncommon in a dovecote of square design, but corner beams overcome its deficiencies to some extent. The largest of all in this group is the rectangular, double, six-gabled dovecote which stands in the grounds of the Manor House Hotel at Lower Slaughter, Gloucestershire. This 16th century building is divided into two chambers, each having its own small Tudor doorway and contains well over 1,000 nests in all. see page 118

Several four-gabled cotes outside Gloucestershire are also of interest. At Langrish Manor Farm in Hampshire, quoins of thin red bricks add striking contrast to the sandstone walls. This dovecote was built at the end of the 15th century, but converted much later to a hop store with the insertion of an extra floor, but many of the stone niches are still preserved. It has recently been well restored. A very fine limestone dovecote of similar date and design, also refurbished recently, stands at Manor Farm, Kelston, Avon. Together with the nearby tithe barns, it originally belonged to the wealthy Benedictine nuns of Shaftesbury Abbey in Dorset. Probably the only one of this type to be found in Sussex is at Trotton, near the Hampshire border. This substantial 17th century structure is built of shaped sandstone blocks with ironstone chips in the mortar, called see page 137

*(top)* Arcaded limestone cote at
Chastleton House
*(bottom)* Dovecote converted to
hop-store, Langrish Manor Farm

see page 120

galleting, and contains almost 1,000 nesting places made of chalk clunch
blocks. At Godminster Manor in Somerset, the lesser but picturesque stone
dovecote has four small main gables which match the cruciform gablets of
its unusual wooden cupola.

Some of these dovecotes have more than one storey. As might be
expected, there are a number of this type in Gloucestershire. Just over the
Oxfordshire border at Chastleton, an elegant limestone cote which carries
a date of 1762 stands alone in a meadow opposite the Elizabethan manor
and church. It has an arcaded ground floor and the upstairs pigeon house
is reached by ladder through a trapdoor. At Greet, a neglected, tall, ashlar

126

A late four-gabled dovecote dated 1917 in the grounds of Abbotswood, Nether Swell

127

An early and probably the only remaining timber-framed dovecote of cruck
construction, at Hill Croome

stone building standing beside the manor house has undergone much interior alteration. However, it seems probable that the upper two-thirds was originally given over to pigeons. A more rugged gritstone rubble building at Llaneugrad on Anglesey contains about 400 nesting boxes in the upper floor.

## Timber Frames

The delightful half-timbered, so-called 'black-and-white' or 'magpie' dovecotes, chiefly to be found nowadays in Herefordshire and Worcestershire are among the most picturesque of all. As is well-known, this form of construction was commonplace early on, particularly in districts without sources of stone, and was used until brick became widely available. Oak was the timber of choice and was generally protected against boring insects by the application of tar, but today other preservatives are used so that the natural colour of the wood is retained, giving a less bold effect which is more brown than black. The infilling varies, but wattle and daub, lath and plaster, stone and brick have all been used. Many of these cotes are built with a plinth of stone on which the timber frame rests. Roofs and cupolas follow several different designs, many having been replaced over the years.

The earliest timber-framed, and probably the sole remaining dovecote of cruck construction, is at Hill Croome in Worcestershire; it dates from the early 15th century. One wall was later replaced by brick and in 1972 the whole structure was dismantled and taken for repair to the Avoncroft Museum of Buildings before being re-erected on its original site. A later timber-framed dovecote at Dormston in the same county has undergone on-site restoration by the same body and now has an altered roof profile.

Restored timber-framed dovecote with altered roof profile at Moat Farm, Dormston

A group of 'black-and-white' dovecotes: *(top left)* White House King's Pyon; *(top right)* Butt House, King's Pyon; *(bottom left)* Hawford Grange, Ombersley; *(bottom right)* Wichenford Court, Worcestershire; *(centre)* later combined water tower and pigeon loft at Plas Newydd, Llangollen

Elsewhere, several other organizations have been involved with preservation. Two dovecotes are under the care of the National Trust, at Hawford Grange, Ombersley, and at Wichenford Court, both in Worcestershire. The charming miniature dovecote at Luntley Court in Herefordshire is an illustration of building a dovecote in advance of the main house, presumably to ensure an immediate supply of food; the dovecote itself is dated 1675, while the house is dated a year later.

see page 138

In Herefordshire, at King's Pyon, the outstandingly attractive three-storeyed dovecote at Butt House is in excellent condition, although the nest-boxes in the top storey, recorded as being present in 1920, have now all gone. It carries the date of 1632 and there has been much conjecture as to its original function, possibly a gatehouse. Local tradition holds that the middle floor was once used as a mews for falcons. If true, they and the pigeons must have been uneasy bed-fellows. The three-storey combined granary and dovecote at Tusmore Park in Oxfordshire is a much larger but more ramshackle building. The pigeons occupied the top, as usual, the grain being stored on both lower floors and the whole building rests on a large number of staddle-stones. Among these timber-framed examples there is an uncommon variation at Dowdeswell in Gloucestershire where the square dovecote, still occupied by white doves, surmounts the arched entrance way to the manor house and stands beside the converted tithe barn and cowshed.

see page 140

see page 139

A much later and relatively modern black-and-white tower at Plas Newydd, Llangollen, Clwyd, appears to have a small pigeon house at its summit and contains a water pump below, for which reason it is usually designated as a water tower. It was probably erected when General Yorke of Erddig bought the house in 1876.

A few survivors have unpainted brick infilling instead of the usual wattle and daub with plaster finish. In the small toy-town dovecote standing in the middle of a field at Pump House Farm, at Hanbury in Worcestershire, coursed red bricks form the plinth and the infilling between the timbers. On the other side of the country at Pimp Hall, Chingford, in Essex, during the course of radical restoration work in 1982, a rougher method using random brick tiles and masonry was found to have been used for the original infilling. This 16th century dovecote is probably the sole remaining timber-framed example in Essex, although many others were still extant as recently as 50 years ago. It no longer contains nesting boxes, nor is there any sign left of the vaulted cellar below ground which once contained a well.

see page 141

see page 142

Wood in the form of weatherboard cladding was much used in early farm buildings of all types, but many have been lost. A few remaining dovecotes of this type, often much restored, illustrate the group. At Northmoor in Oxfordshire, the dovecote with its stone tiled roof and cupola sits above an archway, while at Gate Cottage, Horsenden,

see page 142

Much decorated brick dovecote at Hodnet Hall

Buckinghamshire, the quaint wooden cupola with the enlarged pigeon house below, surmounts the roof of a three-bay wagon shed; it is said to date from the 16th century. Another well-preserved wooden structure is the combined granary and upper pigeon loft at Milford in Surrey. At Malton in Cambridgeshire access for the birds is provided through two ridge gablets in the hipped, tiled roof, but unfortunately the weather-boarded body of the main building is in disrepair.

### Brick Construction

A large number of square and oblong dovecotes were built of brick from the 17th century onwards, most of them in an unremarkable style. Many are still standing, but their distribution varies from county to county. A recent survey of dovecotes in Cambridgeshire, for instance, shows that among a total of 80, almost half were of brick, while in Gloucestershire only four brick ones are to be found among 40 of this type.

In general, roofs, cupolas and flight-holes follow the pattern of other square and oblong dovecotes, but there are several overall variants. At Clifton in Nottinghamshire the double 18th century dovecote, which stands on the village green, is the largest in the county. It contains well over 2,000 nest-holes, but unlike most other dovecotes with two compartments, has only one entrance door. It was restored in memory of those killed in the Second World War and bears a stone plaque with their names. One of the very few oblong brick cotes to have profuse decoration stands at Hodnet Hall in Shropshire and carries the date of 1650 above the door. In addition to bold ashlar stone dressings, it has a line of sunken, diamond-shaped motifs running along each wall above the string course, while

Queniborough dovecote shown
with its 1987 restoration plan. It
was dismantled and moved to a
new site nearby

similar triangular features occupy the two gables. A smaller and less
ornamental pigeon house at Queniborough Hall, Leicestershire, displays
the date of 1705 in raised bricks on an outer wall. Brick finials decorate
both gables and the attractive dormers. The whole fabric was restored in
1987. At Abbey House, Burnham, in Buckinghamshire, the 16th century
square dovecote has walls of 2¼ inch bricks laid in English bond and a
thatched roof, hipped on all sides. The white doves in residence enter
through two wall openings, one of which has a three-centred head. A later
square brick dovecote at the Avoncroft Museum of Buildings in Worcestershire is an interesting and instructive case and is not entirely what it
seems to be on the surface. Several years ago it was removed from
Haselour Hall in Staffordshire and during the dismantling an earlier
timber-framed structure was revealed beneath the brickwork. It is an
example of that fashionable up-dating which transformed many buildings
in the 17th and 18th centuries.

see page 143

133

Seighford Hall. Pigeon tower and game larder attached to gamekeeper's cottage

Many square brick dovecotes of more than one storey still exist. Some are utilitarian in purpose and either stand alone or form part of a continuous range of farm buildings where they are sometimes flanked by, or mounted above, other housing such as stables, cow byres, pigsties, wagon sheds, granaries or smithies. At Kirkley Hall in Northumberland, the squat, battlemented tower on three floors with a lancet-shaped doorway and blocked window, stands between former farm sheds and a cow byre. It now forms part of Northumberland Agricultural College and has been converted into a classroom with modern windows, being much spoilt in the process. Another square Gothic tower at Seighford Hall in Staffordshire is attached to the gamekeeper's cottage. The upper part houses the pigeons, while the ground floor may once have conveniently functioned as a game larder. Other unusual combinations include the use of the lower part as an earth closet, ice-house or mortuary. Some

dovecotes have a more decorative function and occupy prominent sites in gardens or grounds as at Fingringhoe in Essex, where the two-storey dovecote was built to serve additionally as a summerhouse. The ground floor has a domed ceiling and four corner seats in niches, while the upper storey contains 400 nests and is reached from outside by ladder. The building was restored in 1969 at which time it was suggested that a third level below ground was once used as a bear-baiting pit, the spectators watching from the floor above, but there hardly seems to have been room for such a pursuit. Another handsome example in Essex which once stood beside a lake at Holfield Grange, Stisted, also had two storeys and was clearly intended as an ornamental feature. It was unfortunately demolished in 1952.

*(left)* Fingringhoe
(from Donald Smith)
*(right)* Holfield Grange
(from Donald Smith)

see page 143

Most four-gabled dovecotes were either stone or timber-built, but a small number were constructed of brick. One of the largest, at Manor Farm, South Stoke, Oxfordshire, stands near the road and dominates a farmyard along with a handsome brick barn opposite and a small granary on staddle-stones nearby. It is still inhabited by pigeons who enter through large circular openings in the gables. There are 1,500 nests inside, and against the walls at three levels are remains of the uncommon scaffolding walkways which are only found elsewhere in a handful of dovecotes. Another large and impressive building of this type at Shenton Hall, Leicestershire, has an unusual interior central block fitted with nest holes.

see page 144

An·interesting two-storeyed example at Eardisland in Herefordshire, lies in a picturesque setting beside the River Arrow. The upper two-thirds contains 900 nesting places reached by an inner staircase from the smaller ground floor chamber which has windows and a conspicuous but inappropriate porched doorway. The cills of three upper glazed windows are raised six inches or so to allow for access and egress of the birds. The lower part may have been intended originally as a garden room, but later is known to have been used as a dame school.

Although the square base-plan was often used in those dovecotes intended for purely functional purposes, it also lent itself to several decorative variations and this adaptable pattern has continued to be used up until the present day.

136

Fine four-gabled lias limestone dovecote at Kelston in Avon

Miniature dovecote at Luntley Court

138

Timber-framed cote surmounting entrance arch to Dowdeswell Manor

139

Early combined granary and pigeon loft, Tusmore Park

Diminutive dovecote at Pump House Farm, still retaining wooden nesting boxes

141

*(top)* Restored timber-framed dovecote in the grounds of the former Pimp Hall
*(bottom)* Quaint wooden cupola and pigeon loft above three-bay wagon shed,
at Gate Cottage, Horsenden

142

*(top)* Impressive reconstructed dovecote from Haselour Hall, now at the Avoncroft Museum of Buildings. In the background is a large cockpit removed from Bridgnorth
*(bottom)* Very large four-gabled brick dovecote with adjacent granary at South Stoke

143

Two-storeyed brick dovecote beside the River Arrow at Eardisland

## CHAPTER VIII

# Polygonal Varieties

### Origins

The octagonal design is an elegant architectural variation which became popular during the 17th and 18th centuries and was adopted for a number of buildings, both religious and secular. It was not a new concept, however, but the revival of an ancient classical form. One of the earliest surviving octagonal buildings is the lovely Tower of the Winds in Athens, built by the Greeks in 100BC to house a water clock. Nearly two millenia later, at the time of the Greek Revival style in England, it inspired several designs including James Wyatt's Radcliffe Observatory in Oxford and his unexecuted plan for a dovecote at Badger Hall, Shropshire.

From classical times onwards, buildings of this pattern, such as the early Italian baptisteries, were constructed in Europe, culminating in a great revival of interest during the Renaissance. In England, most castle keeps were square in form, but as early as AD1171, King Henry III's masons constructed an octagonal tower at Chilham Castle, Kent which still exists today. In later medieval times the octagon became the prototype for some of our remarkable chapter houses, like those at York Minster and Wells Cathedral. It was not until much later, stimulated by the Renaissance, that the design became widely incorporated into English domestic architecture. This trend coincided with the increasing use of brick in vernacular architecture, with the result that there are more surviving octagonal dovecotes built of brick than of all other materials such as stone, flint and timber, combined.

There are marked regional differences in distribution of this type of dovecote. A Cambridgeshire survey has revealed only two octagonal varieties out of a total of 80 dovecotes, while in Worcestershire it was estimated in 1974 that there were none at all among 64 existing dovecotes. In Donald Smith's classic work on Essex dovecotes, published in 1931, there are 57 dovecotes listed and illustrated, of which only eight are octagonal, while in Nottinghamshire there is only one among 150 dovecotes recently recorded in the county. By contrast, of the small number of remaining dovecotes in Hertfordshire, at least a quarter are octagonal.

Many dovecotes of this design are quite plain, but all are elegant and each differs in one detail or another; the roofs, the cupolas and their finials, the dormers, the cornices, the flight-holes and doors with their

145

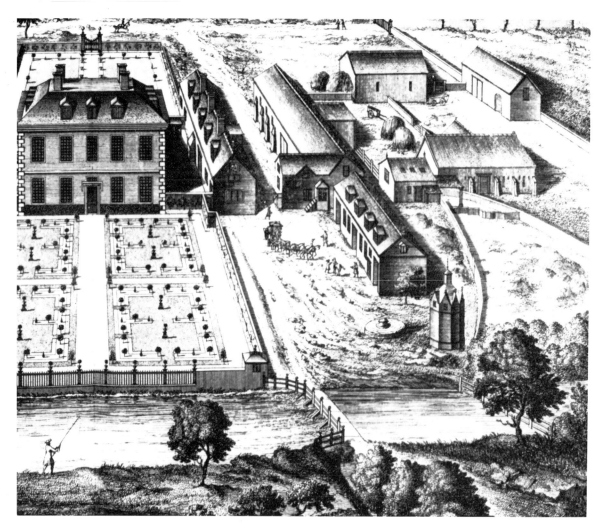

Detail from an 18th century
engraving of the
Manor House, Lower Swell

dressings, all gave scope for individual variation. An 18th century engraving of the Manor House at Lower Swell in Gloucestershire shows an elegant dovecote having eight gables with finials crowded together around the roof parapet. Unfortunately it has disappeared without trace and has no known imitators.

Records reveal that the massive octagonal ashlar stone dovecote at Dallington House in Northamptonshire once had an eight-sided ogee roof of Collyweston slabs, crowned by an octagonal cupola. It was well described by A.O.Cooke in 1920, but had become ruinous by 1972. At Chicheley in Buckinghamshire, the recently restored brick cote has a circular, domed roof which sits strangely on the octagonal base-plan. see page 154 Dormers in the roof are occasional enlivening features. At Erddig in Clwyd, the dovecote has three, while at Little Gaddesden in Hertfordshire the roof supports a record number of eight.

146

Walls are often plain, but the semicircular windows, also described as diocletian, on either side of the door in the 17th century brick cote at Felbrigg, Norfolk, are notable features. At Loxley Hall in Staffordshire, there is a window below the eaves in each of the eight wall segments which make the interior of the building wonderfully light. It has no cupola, but the unglazed lower part of each window allows access for the birds.

see page 155
see page 154

## Stone

A small number of octagonal dovecotes fabricated in stone are widely scattered about the country. At Honington Hall, Warwickshire, described by Pevsner as 'a gem of a late 17th century house', the pale limestone dovecote with contrasting quoins stands alongside the earlier Elizabethan stable block with which it may be contemporaneous. A sundial is mounted on a south wall facing the house. In Oxfordshire, the only remains of Milcombe Hall are fragments of the stables and the elegant grey stone dovecote with four hipped dormers, which stands alone in a field and is clearly visible from the road. It contains traces of a central octagonal stone table. At Sherborne Park, Gloucestershire, the yellow Cotswold limestone dovecote with a low arcaded base now stands in the angle between one end of the house and the stableyard and probably dates from 1750. Also in Gloucestershire, but of earlier date, is the tall ashlar stone example at Frampton Court which belongs to a distinctive cluster of elegant dovecotes all built in the classical mode, as mentioned later. Walls of a rich rubblestone mixture of sandstone, flint and brick joined with brick quoins give a colourful appearance to the cote at Pigeon House Farm at Eastbury in Berkshire. The ochre-coloured marlstone, of which the tower dovecote at Wroxton Abbey, Oxfordshire, is built, together with its Gothic Revival style and architectural attribution, make it an exception, apart from its near neighbour at Idlicote in Warwickshire. This latter, striking neo-Gothic dovecote of grey limestone with brownish quoins is in two storeys, the upper of which, reached by ladder from outside, contains more than 500 brick-built nesting places in linear arrangement. Local legend holds that the structure was moved from Kenilworth Castle to its present site in the 19th century and possibly adapted as a dovecote at that time. The unusual combination of a brick interior with a stone exterior is certainly suggestive.

see page 156

see page 156

see page 157

There are several other individual variations to be found in this two- and three-storeyed group. Also in neo-Gothic style, but of a very different character, is the rubblestone example at Buckland Home Farm, Oxfordshire. This early 19th century building carries much decorative detail, including a mossy vermiculated frieze halfway up and on each face there are blocked pointed arches below and alternating crosslets and

see page 157

147

Dovecote with helm roof at
Wiston Park

quatrefoil recesses above. It may have been built to supply squabs to
nearby Buckland Park which was designed in 1757 by John Wood the
Younger. A smaller, altogether different example is attached to outbuildings at Wiston Park, Sussex. The walls are constructed of ashlar stone on a
flint plinth, the birds being housed in the upper part. The notable feature
is its helm roof which has a truncated tip. Was it based on the famous Saxon
tower of Sompting Church in the vicinity, which has a gabled pyramidal
cap called a 'Rhenish helm' after the German Romanesque churches of the
Rhineland?

There is a group of elegant 18th century ashlar stone dovecotes in the
west, of which two are octagonal. In Gloucestershire, the one at Painswick
House has two storeys and in Avon, the outstanding cote at Widcombe
Manor Farm has three. At the 17th century mansion named The Hall at
Bradford-on-Avon, Wiltshire, the substantial three-storeyed stone
dovecote was converted into a cottage some time ago. All of these must
have belonged to those ornamental garden buildings variously known as
pavilions, gazebos or summerhouses, which often had partial accommodation for the birds.

In addition to their decorative and leisure use, several dovecotes have
been exploited for practical purposes as at Abercamlais, near Brecon,
where the square ground floor of the octagonal superstructure straddles a
stream and once functioned as a latrine. An interesting and imposing
variation in the classical taste is to be found at Exton Park, Rutland, where
the octagonal centre block for pigeons is crowned with eight roof spirelets
and is partly encircled on the ground floor by a most handsome loggia for
cattle.

*(top)* Two-storey cote at Abercamlais,
once housing a latrine below
*(bottom)* Exton Park (see also p.187)

Manor House, Stewkley
showing good diaper work

### Brick

A fair number of brick-built octagonal dovecotes still stand. One of the earliest at Whitehall, Shrewsbury, dates from the end of the 16th century and uses Elizabethan bricks. Its sole decoration is a beautiful arcaded corbel table below the eaves. Many later brick cotes carry a less elaborate dentil or saw-tooth cornice, while low relief or coffered panelling of the walls in the classical style is another form of adornment; a good example is to be seen at Chetwynd in Shropshire. Combined brick and stone provide another ornamental form, as at Dunham Massey in Cheshire, where the ashlar stone quoins contrast with the main walls. Attractive diaper patterns using vitrified header bricks are occasionally used, an excellent example being at Stewkley, Buckinghamshire, and sometimes the dovecote walls repeat the decoration of the main house, as at Compton Wynyates, Warwickshire. Other patterns are simpler and consist merely of alternating colours of brick overall. A very unusual form of brick embellishment is see page 158 to be seen on the dovecote carrying the date 1641 at Hellens, Much Marcle, Herefordshire. Bold geometrical motifs solidly painted in white give a harlequin effect to the walls which is probably unique in the dovecote repertoire.

150

Arcaded, two-storey dovecote in the grounds of Shackleford House

Octagonal brick dovecotes were sometimes built in two stages, of which several are recorded and a few still exist. At Shobdon in Herefordshire, and Loxley Hall in Staffordshire, the upper pigeon house predominates and the space below is now merely used for storage. A similar construction is found at Walkern in Hertfordshire where it is known that the lower storey once functioned as a granary. The building has recently been converted into a cottage. At Shackleford, Surrey, the ornamental garden building has an arcaded undercroft with a granary above, the pigeons apparently being confined to the top floor, but there are no longer any signs of nesting places. This combination of granary and pigeon house is not uncommon, sometimes in the form of separate neighbouring buildings.

151

## Flint and Brick

Flint was combined with brick to decorate several octagonal dovecotes in those districts in which flint occurs naturally. In Sussex, three delightful 18th and 19th century types are situated in the southern part of the county. They have brick quoins and dressings with flint infilling which at Newtimber Place is knapped and coursed; at Coombe Place, blank quatrefoils and arched windows form additional features of the walls, whereas a saw-tooth cornice decorates the one at Bailiffscourt. All contain brick-built nesting places of differing construction and arrangement, including the addition of chalk alighting ledges at Coombe Place. A notable interior detail at Newtimber is the top double row of nests which consist of large circular 'flower-pots' on their sides. In all three, the standard of workmanship is high, both inside and out, and their present condition is excellent. Other larger versions of the flint and brick combination are to be found at Rougham Hall, Norfolk and at Biddesden House, Wiltshire. Inside the latter, full-length tree-trunk posts occupy each angle and were possibly used to attach shelves or supports for nest-boxes, all of which have now gone. Another dovecote of this type in which no nesting places remain is at Firle Place Farm in Sussex.

In districts deficient in building stone, such as Essex, many dovecotes including those of octagonal design were constructed of wood, sometimes in the form of weatherboarding and often on a simple foundation of brick. Writing in 1931, Donald Smith described and illustrated several examples which even at that time were in a parlous condition and probably none has survived.

## Hexagonal and Others

There is a handful of dovecotes which have an hexagonal rather than an octagonal base-plan. Most of them are brick-built, but one very large and impressive exception is constructed of blue lias limestone. This stark grey building stands close to Shapwick House, Somerset, which was built in 1630 for Sir Henry Rolle, the Lord Chief Justice. This may account for the excellent finish of the dovecote. Although the coursed stone walls are plain in the extreme, the square-headed doorway is importantly dressed with ashlar stone. The remarkable interior contains more than 1,000 nests with alighting ledges to each row and an additional wide hexagonal central column also contains nests. In Shapwick the neighbouring manor house possesses a large and more ancient circular dovecote, also built of blue lias. It is rather unusual to find two such substantial dovecotes within a stone's throw of each other, but Sir Henry's house was built at a time when the dovecote was regarded as a status symbol, so perhaps there was an element

152

4 Flint and brick dovecotes: *(top left)* Coombe Place; *(top right)* Firle Place Farm;
*(bottom left)* Newtimber Place; *(bottom right)* Bailiffscourt

*(top left)* Odd effect of a domed roof on an octagonal base, at Chicheley; *(top right)* Erddig
*(bottom left)* Loxley Hall, previously surrounded by stabling; *(bottom right)* Ornamental hexagonal dovecote at Brocton Hall

Felbrigg

155

*(top)* Honington Hall. Early dovecote beside later house
*(bottom)* Milcombe Hall dovecote

156

*(top left)* Pigeon House Farm; *(top right)* Wroxton Abbey dovecote
*(bottom left)* Buckland House Home Farm; *(bottom right)* Idlicote House

157

Harlequin effect at Hellens, Much Marcle

Old Manor, Bradford-on-Avon

159

*(top)* Southstoke Farm, Bath
*(bottom)* Garage at Blockley

160

of keeping up with his neighbour. A smaller stone hexagonal cote of a quite different character is to be found much further north at Forcett Hall, Richmond, in Yorkshire. It was designed in the classical style in the 18th century and has an arcaded ground floor with accommodation for the birds above.

Surviving brick-built hexagonal dovecotes include one at Melbourne Hall, which has been converted into the muniment room, and another at Netherseal Hall, both in Derbyshire. At Buriton, Hampshire, a large plain cote stands beside the manor and is still inhabited by pigeons. Some have more than one floor, for example, at Golding Farm, Pitchford, Shropshire, where a slender two-staged pigeon house now forms part of a range of farm outbuildings. The domed ceiling of the ground floor is unusual and raises the possibility that it was a summerhouse at one time. At Brocton Hall in Staffordshire the tall brick dovecote is lavishly orna- see page 154
mented with Gothic motifs. It stands beside a golf course fairway and has recently been restored with funds raised by members of the club. Amongst the very few with three storeys, the dovecote at Foxley, Yazor, Here- fordshire, is a fine example. Although mainly of brick, the lower walls are made of stone and it was designed to have an ice-house on the ground floor, a game larder in the middle and a dovecote above.

Pentagonal dovecotes are exceedingly rare. There is no doubt that they were built in the past — a ground plan of Holt Castle in Clwyd, dated 1620, shows a five-sided building in the courtyard marked 'decayed dovehouse five square'. The one and only known survivor of this pattern is an elegant, battlemented doocot at Nisbet House in Berwickshire.

Much altered, hexagonal, vaulted dovecote and adjoining piggery at Golding Farm, Pitchford

Steeple Bumpstead, now demolished
(from Donald Smith)

Finally, an early illustration shows an hexagonal garden building which once stood overlooking the lake at Steeple Bumpstead in Essex. It had an arcaded ground floor, above which pigeons were housed; the whole effect must have been singularly ornamental.

# CHAPTER IX

# Pigeon Lofts and Gable Ends

**Lofts**

As far back as Roman times, pigeons were sometimes kept in top storeys or attics of people's homes. These pigeon lofts were often additional to the large separate *columbaria* and the roof-top turrets where birds were bred for the table. Juvenal in his *Satires* describes a loft as 'the place where thy tame pigeons next the tiles were bred' and several other classical writers allude to the custom. The proximity of the birds indoors cannot have been particularly salubrious, but such housing was probably used only for small numbers of the fancy birds which were so popular at the time that Pliny was led to comment: 'Pigeon fancying is carried to insane lengths by some people'.

Over the centuries the meaning given to pigeon loft has changed, but initially it described an upstairs, generally top storey, room or space whose walls were lined with nesting places. Essentially, it formed a subsidiary part of a main building, either a domestic dwelling or one of various outbuildings such as stables, coach houses, cow byres and the wagon entrances of barns. Less commonly, they have been found surmounting privies, dairies, wine cellars, ice-houses, dog kennels and in one case, a donkey house. The most unusual combination to have been recorded was at Balfour Castle on the Island of Shapinsay, in the Orkneys, where the lower part below the pigeon loft was fitted with a salt-water shower and called a 'douche house'.

There are also rarer ecclesiastical versions to be seen. In church towers, the pigeon loft is generally relegated to the middle storey below the belfry, while others are occasionally located in the chancel roof space, as at Elkstone, or above the entrance porch. In the well-preserved three-storeyed chapter house of the Carthusian priory at Hinton Charterhouse, a large pigeon loft is sited above the vaulted middle storey library to which another smaller loft is annexed.

Several domestic lofts have been described. In the recent past an account of Pond House Farm in Upper Beeding, Sussex, written in 1933, mentions the remains of earthenware pot nesting places in the walls of what was once an attic. Today, one of the very few intact pigeon lofts is in the substantial 17th century stone house known as Knabb's Hall near Barnsley in

Church Farm, Leighterton.
Barn loft above wagon entrance

Yorkshire, where square nest boxes of plaster, lath and wood line the inside roof space and walls of the middle attic gable. There is a single entrance for the birds, now blocked, and the loft communicates with the bedroom below. An interesting local variation in which lofts were constructed above the commodious front porches of 17th and 18th century houses in West Yorkshire was first described by A.O. Cooke in 1920. One or more entrance holes were provided for the birds in the main wall and access to the nests was through a trapdoor in the porch ceiling. On a smaller scale, Joseph Gandy's design of 1805 for a cottage includes accommodation for pigeons in an upper loft which is entered through an adjoining bedroom.

Many pigeon lofts incorporated in farm buildings still exist, but it seems likely that numbers of them escape attention, particularly those in which the interior fittings have disappeared. Others have been converted out of all recognition for different uses. Several large well-preserved lofts are still to be found above barn wagon entrances, as for example at Church Farm, Leighterton, Gloucestershire and above coach houses at Luckington Court and Blacklands Park in Wiltshire; the latter is as large as many freestanding dovecotes and contains more than a thousand nests. A recent restoration of the combined pigeon loft and cart shed at Castle Farm, Walworth in Durham is another good example. An unusual feature in the midden yard at Shugborough Hall, Staffordshire, is the circular arrangement of entrance holes to the loft above the salting room. Early in the 19th

164

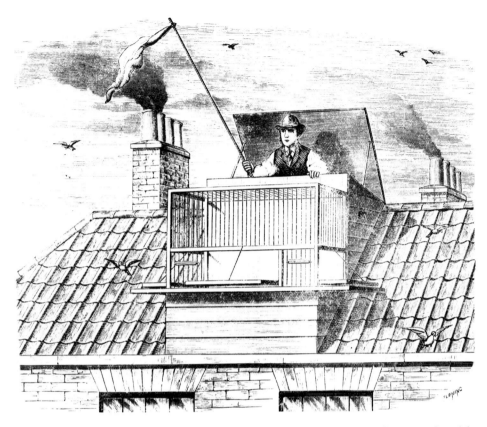

John Moore's recommended loft arrangement!

century, many notable architects turned their attention to farm and stable outbuildings in which lofts were to be incorporated. Two examples, complete with their original plans, illustrate the trend. Ornhams Hall in Yorkshire was designed by J.B.Papworth in 1835 and his plans for the bean barn and pigeon loft in the farmyard are embellished with colour-wash and show details of the pigeon turret and its weathercock. A few decades later, C.F.A.Voysey's plans for Bannut Tree Farm House in Worcestershire, described by Pevsner as his 'first country house job', are also prettily illustrated in watercolour and show two birds perched on the pigeon loft above the stable.

Throughout the 18th century, dovecotes of many different types were being built, but their design was becoming adapted to the changing aspects of pigeon keeping. Small numbers of birds were still bred for eating, but there was increasing emphasis on keeping fancy and racing varieties. Daniel Girton, writing in *The Complete Pigeon Fancier* (1785), alludes to pigeon houses, mostly built of wood, in farmyards, the yards of inns and gentlemen's courtyards, while John Moore in his *Columbarium or the Pigeon House* (1735), largely concentrates on the building of domestic lofts. He recommends, somewhat drastically, that a hole should be made in the roof of the house and describes the trap to be built on the outside for the exit

(*left*) Self-contained cupola loft above cockpit at Bisley, Gloucestershire (*right*) Wooden case on outside wall at Kipling's house in Rottingdean

and entrance of the birds. Moore talks of keeping 'those you breed for the dish' alongside the fancy varieties, but with special precautions to confine the latter so that the strain would be unsullied.

By the end of the century the advantages of the pigeon loft compared with other forms of housing seem to have become firmly established. J.C. Loudon, writing in an *Encyclopaedia of Agriculture* (1835), summarises his views thus:

> *Pigeon houses are of three kinds, small boarded cases fixed on posts, trees, or against the ends of houses; lofts fitted up with holes or nests; and detached buildings. The first are generally too small to contain a sufficient brood, and are also too subject to variations of temperature; and the last, on the other hand, now-a-days too large, and therefore the most suitable for the farmer is a loft or tower rising from a building...*

The use of an enlarged cupola, sealed off at the base, as a loft or miniature dovecote was one version which was widely adopted and many are still to be seen above farm and garden buildings. The ample cupola on the ashlar stone cockpit at Bisley in Gloucestershire is an uncommon combination, while the wooden version replacing the cowl and vent of an oasthouse at Bateman's, Sussex, is another. Loudon's mention of exterior wooden cases hung on outside walls or poised on poles is a reference to another form of housing which, although he condemns it, has continued in use until the present day. A current resurgence of interest in this type of 'loft' is reflected in the glossy magazines which proclaim that 'romantic dovecotes and their inhabitants are a beautiful addition to a garden'.

166

*(top)* A general loft of 1893
*(bottom left)* Elegant 'barrel-on-a-pole'
loft in the Pet's Cemetery at
Longleat House
*(bottom right)* 1987 version of
miniature loft at
Trueleigh Manor, Upper Beeding

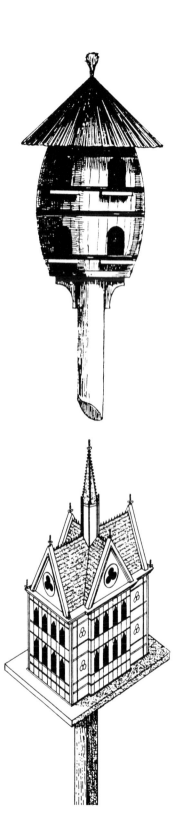

Lofts underwent a final transformation during the latter part of the 19th century, largely in answer to the tremendous popularity of fancy and racing pigeon breeding. They no longer occupied upper storeys, but were built on the ground in backyards and gardens and became more like sheds or aviaries in construction. Special entrance traps were fitted and in addition to the customary nesting boxes they were provided with mating and separating compartments and special drinking and feeding devices. A rather different 20th century development was the use of mobile military lofts to house carrier pigeons during both World Wars.

## Gables and Walls

Another arrangement provides accommodation for pigeons in the outside walls and gables of various buildings. It comprises several rows of holes with a variable number of alighting ledges which lead to nesting recesses built within the thickness of the walls. In contrast to the single or small number of entrance holes in lofts and dovecotes, these external niches sometimes total more than a hundred. Lofts and gable nesting places were sometimes complementary to freestanding dovecotes, as has been shown by recent studies in lowland Staffordshire and north-east Wales, where housing in lofts and walls outnumbers the separate cotes still existing. This is probably true in many other parts of Britain; exterior nest-holes, in particular, are ubiquitous in rural buildings of all kinds and for this reason are often ignored although some are worth recording. However, they must be distinguished from the square 'breather' or ventilation holes, often arranged in patterns and found in the walls of barns and granaries.

This type of housing may have been devised to save space or cost; it was undoubtedly a widespread custom and not confined to this country. The 15th century Italian painting of the Annunciation by Crivelli depicts an early Renaissance version with unusual multiple perching rods.

In the remaining buildings of the Norman priory on Caldey Island in South Wales, several rugged, square nesting niches on the inner wall of the courtyard are situated alongside several others above the ancient gateway. Such accommodation would hardly have housed enough birds to provide food for the early monastic community, but there is no longer any sign of a freestanding dovecote. On the other hand, a large number of exterior nesting holes is to be seen in an 18th century engraving of Hyde Abbey, Winchester, originally a Benedictine nunnery, of which only the medieval gatehouse remains. This illustration shows tiers of niches and alighting ledges covering the entire surface of one visible wall of the square church tower. If the other two elevations were similarly furnished, a sizeable number of squabs could have been available for the nuns' refectory.

The openings of wall and gable nest-holes vary from the crude to the

Detail from Crivelli's 'Annunciation', showing gable nests and perching poles (15th century)

A variety of loft arrangements:
*(top left)* Rowley Grange,
Farleigh Hungerford;
*(top right)* Blaise Hamlet, Bristol;
*(bottom left)* Barton Farm;
*(bottom right)*
Methuen Arms, Corsham

see page 159

ornate. At Barton Farm in Bradford-on-Avon, Wiltshire, the pigeon-holes are situated prominently on the main wall of the house and are unusual in having pointed arches. Elsewhere, exterior holes also lend decorative effect as can be seen in the white wooden gables of two cottages in John Nash's picturesque model village of Blaise Hamlet near Bristol and on a smaller scale in two garden houses at Kempsey in Worcestershire and at the Old Manor in Bradford-on-Avon .

Innumerable straightforward examples are still to be found in farm-houses, cottages, stables, outbuildings and inns. There are also some puzzling variations as, for example, the four-gabled stone building of characteristic Cotswold design at Horsley Manor in Gloucestershire. The exterior appears to be a typical dovecote, but there is no summit cupola and each gable is completely filled by a single large circular orifice surrounded by several rows of square nest-apertures and alighting ledges;

170

the interior lacks any trace of nesting accommodation. It turns out that the building was originally constructed as a granary with subsidiary housing for pigeons in the outer gable walls. The large holes are thought to have provided access for owls to prey on vermin within.

*(left)* Cottage at Duntisbourne Leer
*(right)* Garden House combination at Squires Close, Kempsey

## Combinations

The combination in one building of typical interior nest construction, either in a loft or single storey dovecote, together with exterior niches in its gables or walls is an occasional and interesting variant. A large many-gabled 16th century stone barn at Southstoke Farm, near Bath, provides a prime example. Several tiers of holes and ledges appear prominently on its two main aspects and in addition there are interior nesting places within the two gable walls of its upper chamber which is reached by an interior stairway. At Kelmscott Manor Farm in Oxfordshire the rows of exterior holes with individual ledges are confined to one gable of the freestanding dovecote, whose cupola gives the birds access to the usual interior nests.

see page 160

171

Dovecote at Hygga Farm,
Trellesey, photographed in 1929

Exterior accommodation on a larger scale is to be found in the circular red sandstone dovecote at Hygga Farm, near Llanishen, Gwent. The upper part of the wall is ringed with six horizontal ledges having spaced vertical divisions between which are numerous pigeon holes; these complement the niches within. Probably the most exceptional dovecote offering alternative forms of housing for birds is the 18th century octagonal three-storeyed tower of ornamental design at Manor Farm, Widcombe in Bath. It has a top-storey loft containing almost 150 nests and nearly as many external recesses in linear ranks on three adjacent walls of the middle storey.

see page 193

A few gable and wall nesting places continue to be incorporated in some present-day buildings. One modern version at Blockley in Gloucestershire combines a ground-floor garage with pigeon-holes in the window gable and others in the form of a cupola. The building was designed by T. Rayson, a local architect, and gained a Civic Award in 1959.

see page 160

# CHAPTER X

# Architectural Flights of Fancy

Early dovecotes were intended solely for the purpose of farming pigeons and were built according to local tradition and without overmuch architectural pretension. However, already in the 16th century the much-travelled Tudor physician, Dr Andrew Boorde, appears to have regarded the dovecote as an ornamental diversion rather than as an adjunct to the kitchen: 'The country gentleman's residence is not complete without a dovecote, a payre of buttes for archery and a bowling alley'. It was not until the beginning of the 18th century, however, that their decorative potential was fully recognized, particularly in those which were incorporated in the newly fashionable landscaped gardens of the period. At that time, it was also common practice to build or disguise utilitarian buildings with elegant façades and site them as eyecatchers in the grounds. A quite different group includes those dovecotes which were placed beside farm and stable outbuildings. From the time of the Enclosures onwards these complexes received increasing architectural attention and this continued well into Victorian times.

These newer dovecotes were sometimes designed by local self-styled architects who often combined their work as builder with that of statuary mason. In others, the owner or patron took it upon himself to direct operations with pattern book in hand. In addition, there are many unusually handsome dovecotes still standing which were designed or embellished by eminent architects and this trend has been followed, although to a diminishing degree, until the present day.

**Palladio in Italy**

In this rather commonplace aspect of their work, the architectural fraternity had a most venerable example in Palladio, the great 16th century Italian Renaissance master, who recognised the dovecote as being not only a practical requirement, but an important feature in the overall architectural composition. An English edition of his work published in 1721 includes dovecotes in several of his designs for what have been called 'country houses for the residence of opulent persons'. These beautiful villas in northern Italy, although built for the wealthy as rural retreats,

173

Four designs by Palladio, incorporating paired dovecotes in the form of terminal pavilions

174

were based on the old Venetian farm system and were intended to be run as self-sufficient units. Each establishment consisted of a nucleus for the owner and his family, together with the farmer's buildings which included stables, barns, cowhouse, dovecote and other outliers. In his text, Palladio paid particular attention to the accommodation for the farm stock: 'All breeding creatures such as hogs, sheep, pigeons, fowl and the like require each a place proper to their kind'. Not a particularly exceptional precept, but it is altogether surprising to find that he singled out dovecotes for prominence in the main façade of several mansions. As Palladio himself puts it in one design, '...at each end of which there is a pigeon house which beside the ornament to the place, likewise brings profit to the owner'. They were generally sited in pairs equidistantly on each side of the villa to which they were connected by elegant covered arcades. At the Villa Maser, near Asolo, noted for its marvellous interior decorations by Veronese, each of the paired dovecotes is two-storeyed; the pigeons were housed above and a wine press was situated below.

In this country, John Wood the Elder came closest to imitating Palladio's penchant for highlighting pigeon houses in the architectural scheme. At Prior Park, near Bath, he planned a combined dovecote, barn and stables in the western wing, the corner pavilion of which he described as being 'partly for coaches to stop under and partly for pigeons to reside in'. Unfortunately, both winged blocks of the Palladian mansion have been altered unrecognizably over the years, but the print by Walker, dated 1754, shows the square dovecote with roof cupola surmounting a grand archway. Few other details exist, but Wood's own comments suggest that he was pleased with the arrangement:

> ...the Pigeons are magnificently Housed...so that if a Beautiful Habitation is really an Allurement to this Species of Birds, as some pretend, Mr Allen's Pigeons will, in all Probability, never desert their present Place of Abode.

An earlier follower of Palladio in this country was Inigo Jones, born in 1573, who has been described as our first true architect. Very few examples of his domestic architecture have been preserved, although many attributions have been claimed, including an octagonal ashlar stone dovecote attached to the mansion at Hutton-in-the-Forest, Cumbria.

## Architectural Attributions in England

In 18th century England, many dovecotes were built in the classical style in the grounds of several mansions both great and small. Architectural attribution is certain for some and strongly suggestive in others.

see page 194

see page 193

see page 194

see page 194

In Wiltshire, John Wood the Elder designed Belcombe Court in 1734 and he was probably responsible for the unusual dovecote which stands in the open courtyard beside the house. It is a stone-built low circular tower with a domed roof and cupola, and surmounts an archway decorated with a bust in the classical style. It presents a striking counterbalance to the beautiful front elevation of the adjacent house.

Not very far away at Widcombe in Bath an elegant three-storeyed octagonal dovecote of ashlar Bath stone stands in the grounds of what was originally the manor farm. The manor, built in 1727, is outstandingly attractive even in a district full of distinguished Georgian houses and the dovecote itself might be justifiably regarded as the quintessence of all others in elegance and ingenuity of design. Today, its idyllic setting in beautiful grounds bounded by meadows and green hills sets off its attraction to perfection. The two lower floors are connected by an interior spiral stone staircase and are both fitted with fireplaces. They were probably intended as garden rooms, the middle floor making a fine belvedere or prospect room with its two windows and window-seats. The top floor contains 150 stone nesting places and can be reached through the ceiling of the middle floor or by ladder from outside. An unusual feature is the provision of the same number of niches in three outside walls of the middle storey. The architect of Widcombe Manor, who almost certainly influenced the dovecote design, is not known, but Thomas Greenway, a local mason and sculptor who worked with John Wood, has been suggested. The name of John Strahan, the well-known Bristol architect and contemporary of Wood, has also been postulated. It may be coincidence that he is linked with two other Palladian houses in the district, both of which have outstandingly handsome dovecotes.

The central part of Painswick House in Gloucestershire is very much in the style of John Strahan and has often been attributed to him. The ashlar stone dovecote with its rusticated square base, arcaded on three sides, has an octagonal upper floor which originally housed the birds. It is conspicuously situated in full view of the house. The ground floor is fitted with a vaulted ceiling, coffered panelling on the walls and a patterned stone floor. Its deep corner recesses with seats in three angles confirm that it was at some time used as a summerhouse. Restoration of the building, together with attractive Gothic outliers in the rococo garden have been carried out according to the painting by Thomas Robins, the Limner of Bath, which depicts the original layout of this enchanting small estate.

Frampton Court in Gloucestershire, built between 1731 and 1733, is believed by some authorities also to have been designed by John Strahan. The tall, octagonal single storey dovecote is in a restrained classical style. The interior walls are entirely fitted with pigeon niches which are still occupied by birds. An ornamental escutcheon in stone forms an attractive detail above one of the two entrance doors. An early photograph shows

176

that glazing bars in a Gothic pattern formerly embellished the pretty cupola and a previously existing dormer window; some of this decoration still remains on both doors.

Apart from this group in the west, a more rugged and recently well-restored dovecote in the classical style is to be found in the north at Forcett Hall, near Richmond in Yorkshire. This hexagonal two-storey dovecote with an arcaded ground floor for sheltering animals was designed and built by Daniel Garnett in the mid-18th century. He was a London-trained, local architect, once a protégé of Lord Burlington, and produced the first publication devoted entirely to farmhouse design.

In the Midlands there is an unusual dovecote at Apethorpe Hall, Northamptonshire. It was built in 1740 and a detailed agreement between the Earl of Westmorland and the local mason is preserved. The oddly shaped dome which arises from the centre of the roof and tops a plain rubblestone circular base suggests a valiant attempt to follow the fashionable trend, perhaps inspired by the patron's pattern books.

Distant view of classical temple incorporating stable and dovecote, at Barrington Park

An imposing 18th century dovecote built as a classical temple in the Pantheon style, stands at a focal point in the landscaped grounds of Barrington Park, Gloucestershire. It is built of local ashlar stone and has an Ionic tetrastyle portico attached to the main circular structure. The highly-domed roof must have originally been crowned by a different cupola access for the birds. It is reported that there are two storeys within, a stable on the ground floor connected by a spiral staircase to the upper pigeon house. The imposing mansion, the grounds and the dovecote have been ascribed to William Kent who, apart from his architectural genius, led the trend away from formal garden design to what was called 'the amiable simplicity of unadorned nature'. There is little evidence to support this attribution, however, and present opinion favours the architect William Smith of Warwick. A few miles away at Rousham, in Oxfordshire, William Kent is known to have planned the grounds with their well-known grottoes, ruins and temples, but there was no need for a new dovecote there. The existing rose-garden already contained a large plain circular one with an attractive cupola and latticed dormer windows, which still stands in the centre today.

At Fenstanton in Cambridgeshire, there was once an unusual brick-built tower dovecote said to have been copied from an Italian original and reputed to have been designed by the son of Lancelot (Capability) Brown in 1780. This may be valid, because Capability Brown retired to a small estate in the district and is buried in the church at Fenstanton. The tower was 50 feet high and is believed to have housed more than 2,000 birds. It collapsed in about 1930, but an early photograph has fortunately been preserved. A cryptic and partly illegible note on the reverse reads: 'About 1805 an Admiral is said to have supplied Navy with ??? pigeons a year'. It seems to have been an enterprising arrangement, but it is a pity that the details are so scanty.

In the early 19th century an existing dovecote was converted into a Doric temple at Corby Castle, Cumbria. In 1813 both it and the mansion were redesigned in the fashionable style by Peter Nicholson, who was County Surveyor and a leading local architect. The cote of deep red ashlar sandstone is square in plan and has a tetrastyle portico and a roof pediment embellished with finials and urns. An inscription 'A quella chi lo merita' on the frieze above the portico capitals is said to be in memory of the death of the owner's Italian fiancée. It has been postulated that the present square dovecote replaced an earlier circular or octagonal one, because the interior potence, a device usually confined to these shapes of dovecote, still survived at the time of the conversion.

In Scotland a few notable architects were involved with dovecote design in the 18th century. In Argyllshire, one of the very few to have been built in that region still stands today at Inveraray Castle. The dovecote was designed in 1748 by William Adam, father of Robert Adam, together with Roger Morris; their working drawings for what is known as the Carloonan dovecote are still preserved. It is a circular tower of two storeys situated at a distance from the main house in a meadow terminating a vista. The lower

The Carloonan Dovecote, Inveraray, by William Adam and Roger Morris

Robert Mylne's unexecuted design for renovation in 1776

181

Henham Hall dovecote, believed to have been designed by James Wyatt, demolished a few decades ago

floor comprises a vaulted chamber with a fireplace and was probably used as a garden room. A decade or two after the dovecote had been built, Robert Mylne was commissioned to update it in the fashionable style. His drawings show the original tower clad with a portico and a domed roof, the whole dovecote being neatly and economically transformed into a classical temple. It is a striking demonstration of the conversion of a building in the current style, nowadays often referred to as façadism. In the event, the commission was not executed and so the dovecote remains in its original state.

In the 18th century not all dovecotes with architectural pretension followed the classical style. An opposing trend from the middle of the century onwards was the school of Gothic Revival which played such an important part in that offshoot of the Romantic movement known as the

Picturesque. At Wroxton Abbey in Oxfordshire, Sanderson Miller designed several features within the park in 1744, of which only the yellow marlstone dovecote remains. It is built in the form of an octagonal, battlemented tower, complete with arrow-slits and quatrefoil decorations. Restoration work has included the replacement of the battlements and a beautiful locally-wrought weathervane. An imaginative fund-raising campaign, in which local people and students in the house were invited to contribute the sum of five pounds per nest-hole enabled the work to be done. A few miles away at Idlicote House, Warwickshire, the tall stone octagonal dovecote in neo-Gothic style bears a marked resemblance to the one at Wroxton Abbey, but unfortunately it has neither firm date of construction nor architectural attribution.

A photograph taken at Henham Hall in Suffolk shows a plain brick-built octagonal dovecote with an elegant stone cupola in Gothic style. It is believed to have been designed by James Wyatt, who was the architect of the main house in the years 1793-7. Unfortunately, both buildings were demolished a few decades ago.

The grounds of Badminton House, Gloucestershire, were much embellished at the end of the 18th century for the fourth Duke by the erstwhile astronomer, landscape gardener and architect Thomas Wright. He used the neo-Gothic style for many outlying farm buildings on the estate, including the massive and extraordinary Castle Barn. It consists of a central block, comprising barn and cowhouse which is flanked by a pair of square battlemented, fort-like towers whose top floors are lined with brick-built nesting places for pigeons.

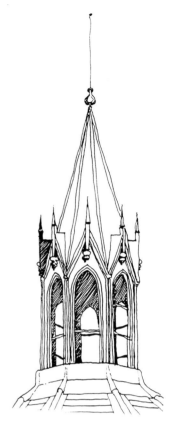

Castle Barn, Badminton, designed by Thomas Wright. Pigeon lofts are in the twin towers

183

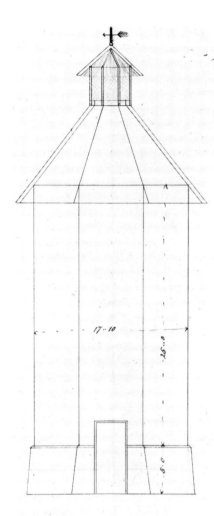

The chinoiserie style was an exotic architectural taste in the 18th century, but few dovecotes of this type have survived. There is a proposal for one in a John Adam sketchbook, but the only existing example, which resembles a Chinese pagoda, stands at Cardross in Perthshire. There are a few illustrative records showing dovecotes of this genre. A painting of Kilkerran House in Ayrshire depicts a pagoda-like dovecote standing in a field with the house in the background, while two unidentified drawings, claimed to be set in the Home Counties, show views of a house with a garden containing a Gothic summerhouse and a large dovecote in the form of a thatched pagoda. There is a suggestion that Sanderson Miller might have been involved with the design of both these ornamental structures.

## Plans and Pattern Books

Several drawings for dovecotes by well-known 18th century architects have been preserved, but only one of them is known to have been executed and it still stands at Little Gaddesden, Hertfordshire. The plan was prepared by Sir Jeffrey Wyattville who, together with his uncle James Wyatt, designed nearby Ashridge Park, that largest of 19th century neo-Gothic mansions near London. The red brick octagonal dovecote, which may have supplied birds to the household, has been much altered by the addition of eight dormer windows and more recently by conversion to a dwelling house.

Although not executed, several other drawings and plans exist which are of interest, particularly the design for an octagonal dovecote at Badger Hall, Shropshire, by James Wyatt, dated 1780. It is based on the Tower of the Winds in Athens and includes elegant ornamental details in the Greek Revival style. If built it would have been an extremely attractive addition to the dovecote repertoire. Samuel Wyatt, another member of the large Wyatt family, worked in the late 18th century at Kedleston, Derbyshire, under Robert Adam who designed not only the magnificent mansion, but also made several plans for a model home farm, many of which were abandoned. This was also the fate of Wyatt's design for a Tuscan cowhouse-cum-dovecote which is one of his earliest surviving drawings. It is square in plan and the open ground floor loggia for cows which encircles the base of the building is most unusual, but is also a striking feature of the handsome octagonal stone dovecote which still stands at Exton Park, Rutland. An illustration of a similar arrangement dated 1778 is to be found among the drawings and designs by Robert and James Adam held in Sir John Soane's Museum, London. This shows an octagonal two-storeyed dovecote encircled by eight columns on the upper stage and an arcaded loggia at ground level. An unexecuted plan for a circular dovecote

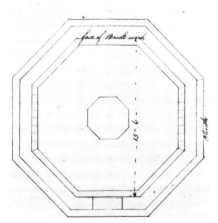

Wyattville's design for the surviving Little Gaddesden dovecote

184

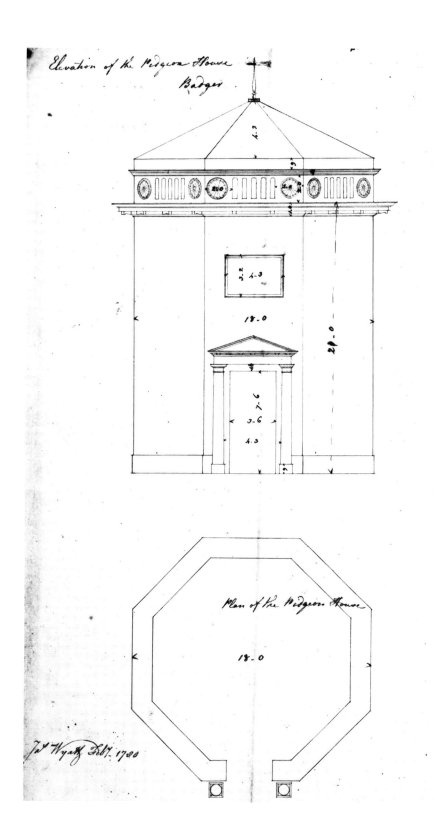

*Elevation of the Pidgeon House Badger*

*Plan of the Pidgeon House*

Jas Wyatt Feb.y 1780

James Wyatt's unexecuted design for a dovecote at Badger Hall based on the Greek 'Tower of the Winds'

185

# Design of a Pigeon House

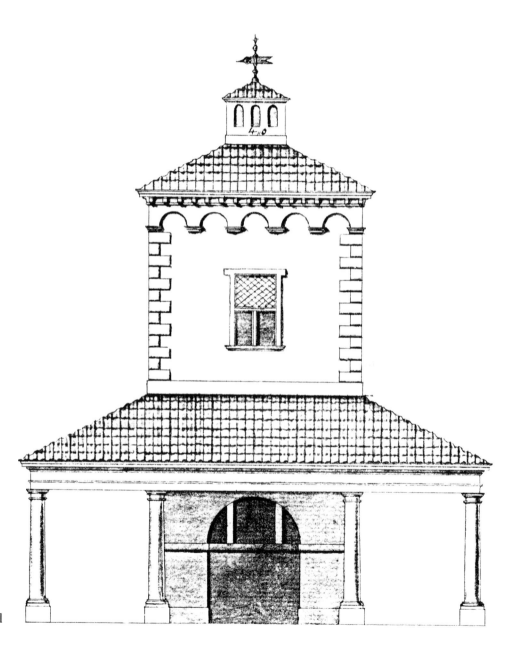

Samuel Wyatt's unfulfilled
design for a Tuscan cowhouse-
cum-dovecote at Kedleston Hall

186

*(top)* Frontal view of Exton Park showing loggia for cattle
(see also p.149)
*(bottom)* 2 dovecote designs by Robert and James Adam, 1778

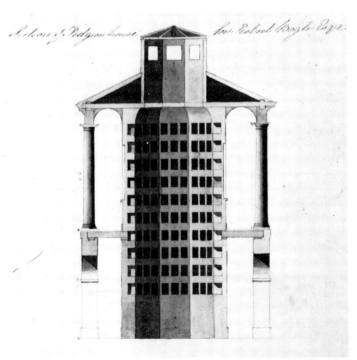

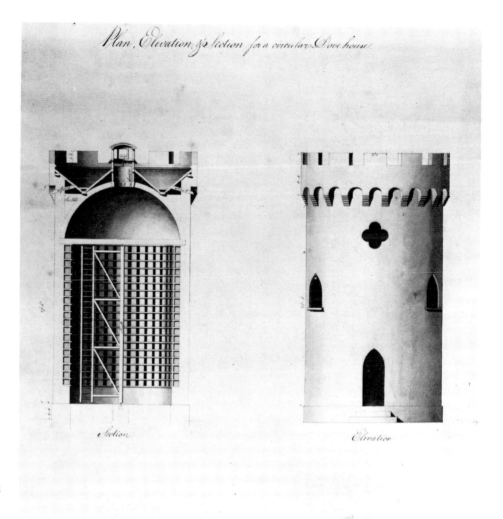

*Plan, Elevation, & Section for a circular Dove house.*

*Section*                *Elevation*

Drawing by James Smith for a
proposed dovehouse at
Coppice Green, 1784

in a pronounced Gothic battlemented style at Coppice Green, Shropshire,
is signed by James Smith who was a local architect and surveyor in
Shrewsbury in the late 18th century.

Many pattern books of the time contained plans for various farm
outbuildings, but only a very few include dovecotes. A fanciful example is
illustrated in the *Modern Builder's Assistant* by William and John Halfpenny,
Robert Morris and Thomas Lightoler amongst pictures and plans for
middling-sized country residences, brewhouses, kennels, dairies and
summerhouses. Their strange design for a dovecote resembles a light-
house and must have been intended largely for decoration. Containing
relatively few nest-holes, the long steep climb to the top, presumably by
ladder, would have been too daunting for more than occasional visits;
perhaps it was for fancy pigeons. There is no record to show that it was
ever built.

Fanciful design by William
Halfpenny, from an 18th century
pattern book

Massive dovecote at Chillington Hall, possibly by Francis Smith

## Farm and Stable Ranges and Courtyards

From the 18th century onwards there was an increasing tendency to group farm buildings and stables together in neat layouts, often arranged as courtyards. Dovecotes were sometimes placed in the centre of the yard, but more often they stood adjacent to, abutting or above another building. Lavish attention was sometimes devoted to these complexes and several notable architects were involved in their design. An impressive existing example is the vast farm and stable courtyard at Chillington Hall, Staffordshire, in which a large octagonal dovecote occupies a central position. The mansion was designed by Francis Smith of Warwick and

several of the dovecote features carry his imprint. Unfortunately, the elaborate glazed cupola has had to be removed temporarily, following recent storm damage; its size and construction are impressive as it stands on the ground alongside.

A smaller, octagonal brick cote abuts a range of stables in the courtyard of the former Hothfield Place in Kent, but its conversion to a dwelling along with the other buildings is imminent. The original complex is thought to have been designed by James Wyatt in 1778. At Cornwell Manor in Oxfordshire a plain square stone dovecote stands in the centre of the stableyard. Its conspicuous tall wooden glover of unusual design may have been added in 1939 when Clough Williams Ellis carried out extensive improvements to the house and gardens.

Cricket House at Cricket St Thomas, Somerset, was designed and built between 1801 and 1804 for Lord Bridport by Sir John Soane who also prepared plans in 1807 for a two-storeyed combined granary and pigeon house. As executed, the present brick building forms the central part of one range of the farm courtyard, but in a modified wedge-shaped form. It is no longer used for either of its original purposes, but has been adapted as part of an agricultural museum.

Many of these outlying buildings continued to receive special attention throughout the 19th century, concepts ranging from the grandiose to the

Stableyard complex at Hothfield Place, by James Wyatt

191

*Monastic Farm*

*(left)* Dovecote as a central feature of a 'monastic farm' by John Plaw *(right)* Tower dovecote in combination with hen house and dog kennels at North Laiths Farm

more modest and restrained. In John Plaw's collection of designs called *Rural Improvements*, published about 1800, a large central dovecote dominates the courtyard of a monastic farm which he describes as being 'to unite the useful with the agreeable'. A contemporary publication, *The Country Gentleman's Architect* by R. Lugar, contains plans for farmhouses, farmyards and stables and includes a dovecote within the curtilage of a farm, flanked by a henhouse, dog kennels and a piggery. Such a combination has been largely realised at North Laiths Farm, Nottinghamshire, where a circular tower dovecote in high Victorian style is fronted by a three-storeyed pedimented façade with arched openings leading to dog kennels and a henhouse on the lower floors.

192

Widcombe Manor Farm

*(top left)* Belcombe Court; *(top right)* Frampton Court; *(bottom)* Painswick House

Courtyard dovecotes: *(top left)* Pednor Farm, Buckinghamshire;
*(top right)* Shipley, Derbyshire; *(bottom)* Wrexham Road Farm, Eccleston, Cheshire

195

Bemerton Farm

Nymans

*(top left)* Ornamental dovecote and clock tower at Cliveden; *(top right)* Wycliffe Hall
*(bottom)* Elizabethan gatehouse pair of dovecotes at Hamstall Ridware

*(top)* The Slipper House and Hermit's House, Bawburgh
*(bottom)* Eyre's Folly, Pepperbox Hill

Dovecote conversions at Haslingfield; Little Gaddesden; Manor Farm, Walkern; and Woolavington

In the mid-19th century, W. Eden Nesfield built an ornamental model farm at Shipley Park in Derbyshire. The house, of earlier date, has vanished and the farm suffered greatly from mining subsidence, but it has recently been restored. The farm buildings are arranged on three sides of a courtyard and include a dairy in the form of a medieval baptistery and a tall Gothic tower which was almost certainly a dovecote. Unfortunately, it no longer contains nesting niches, but the dormers seem to form typical access openings for the birds.

see page 195

The architect John Douglas built several attractive model farms on the Duke of Westminster's estate in Cheshire towards the end of the 19th century. Several of these have pigeon lofts, but at Wrexham Road Farm a small freestanding brick tower dovecote with a weatherboarded turret stands in an angle of the courtyard.

At Madresfield, Worcestershire, the towering circular brick dovecote, which was restored by Norman Shaw in 1867, stands beside the cow byre. He embellished it with an unusual stone 'château dormer' which is mounted high on the outside wall above the door. It contains rows of flight-holes and a two-light window and enlivens an otherwise unexceptional building.

Probably the most modern dovecote to be built in the centre of a courtyard is at Pednor Farm in Buckinghamshire. In 1911 Edwin Forbes enlarged and converted a three-sided farm courtyard into a stylish country house. At the same time he built the neat circular dovecote which is still occupied by birds today, although he failed to provide any nesting places.

Combined pigeon and poultry house at Blencowe

201

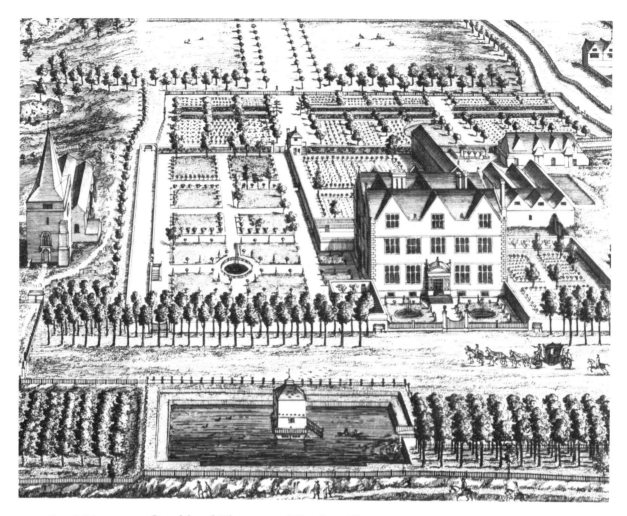

Aquatic dovecote at Sundridge
Park; pigeons above, ducks below
(detail from Kip's engraving)

## Combined Pigeon and Poultry Houses

The novel idea of housing together 'ground and winged game' was
introduced at a time when the large pigeon house was already in decline. A
romantic Greek Revival design for a building to house doves and hens is
included in a work on ornamental gardening produced in 1823 by John
Buonarotti Papworth, the architect who is chiefly known for his work in
Cheltenham; whether it was ever executed is not known. An intriguing
variation of such combined accommodation is depicted in Kip's engraving
of Sundridge Place, Kent, where a building in the middle of a lake housed
ducks on the watery floor and pigeons in the top storey. The middle floor
with a balcony served as a summerhouse and was reached by boat from the
shore and thence by a flight of steps.

At Blencowe, Cumbria, an elegant little two-storeyed building, dated
1789, houses three sizes of bird; hens and geese or turkeys occupy two sizes

202

Cilwendeg dovecote, built in 1835

of nest on the ground floor while there are pigeon niches above. Another much larger and more elaborate combined poultry and pigeon house on three floors, dated 1835, forms part of the home farm at Cilwendeg, near Boncath, Dyfed. This impressive building with a square central tower, flanked by two linked wings has been described as a confection of slate and stone; notable features include the generous provision of slate sunning ledges on the outer walls. Pigeons were kept in the upper chamber, turkeys and hens on the middle floor and ducks and geese enjoyed running water in a channel on the ground floor. Slate nest boxes graded appropriately to the size of the inhabitants are found within. At Bemerton Farm, Wiltshire, a circular tower together with other outbuildings was constructed in idiosyncratic style in 1850. A pair of stepped stone ramps may have provided an entrance for hens, while two rows of pigeon flight-holes pierce the upper wall. It has several quaint Gothic features and the strange hagstone walls are described by Pevsner as 'terrible crazy paving'. The style is said to have been copied from a Russian farm and was built to please a Russian countess, the owner at that time.

see page 196

203

## Cottage Dovecotes

Farm workers were decently housed on many landed estates during the 18th century, often as a result of ambitious rebuilding schemes. Elsewhere they often endured appalling living conditions largely due to the acute shortage of rented accommodation. Stirrings of conscience eventually led to widespread moves to provide them with better homes. At the same time there was a pressing need higher up the social scale for up-to-date farmhouses for the new breed of aspiring tenant farmers. Architects and designers were quick to exploit both these demands and a profusion of pattern books appeared. Many of them concentrated on the more modest rural buildings, as for example Joseph Gandy's work entitled *Designs for Cottages, Cottage Farms and Rural Buildings*, published in 1805. Some of his designs are a trifle fanciful, but unlike those of his contemporaries who emphasized the place of the pigsty in the cottage economy, he concentrated on the keeping of pigeons. Several cottages include accommodation for the birds in integral lofts upstairs with access through the ceiling of the room below. One example, however, shows a circular dovecote contiguous with the cottage which is described as being 'adapted for the Breed of Pigeons for Sale'. Breeding pigeons for the table was no doubt familiar to everyone at this time and a steady supply of birds must have reached the market from sources such as this.

## Modern Concepts

Early in his career, the great Edwin Lutyens made drawings for a very jolly fowl-house with pigeon loft at Littleworth Cross in Surrey. It was one of his earliest ventures in collaboration with Gertrude Jekyll who herself did much to create a revival of interest in the use of dovecotes in garden design. Her book on garden ornament, published in 1918, features several of her choices, both old and new. At this time, few new dovecotes were being built, largely because the need for pigeon meat had greatly dwindled, but a lingering tradition to have one in the garden seems to have persisted; perhaps the idea of white doves fluttering about had an aesthetic appeal. However, most of these modern examples were built on a much smaller scale than hitherto.

see page 198

At Cliveden, in Buckinghamshire, the neo-Classical mansion built by Sir Charles Barry in 1850 was embellished shortly afterwards by Henry Clutton. He added a clock tower and an ornamental dovecote, both in contrasting flamboyant Victorian style, which stand facing each other across the entrance courtyard.

In Gloucestershire there is a diminutive wall-mounted stone dovecote in each of the gardens of two houses built at Sapperton in 1901 by Ernest

Gimson and Sidney Barnsley who were moving spirits in the Arts and Crafts movement in vogue at the time. The small circular cote at the house called Beechanger, which Barnsley built for himself, is furnished with a menacing ring of metal teeth below the nest-boxes, a remnant from the past when similar devices were used to discourage marauders. Both these little structures bear a striking resemblance to the earlier and larger example at Harlyn House, St Merryn, in Cornwall, which has much in common with the Mediterranean pillar dovecotes.

*(left)* Beechanger, Sapperton
*(right)* Attractive modern design by George Crawley at Crowhurst Place

205

see page 197

see page 198

In the 1920s, Sir Walter Tapper designed a house in medieval style for Colonel Messel at Nymans in Sussex. Described by Pevsner as 'this amazingly deceptive evocation of a major manor house of the 14th-16th century', it has a pretty circular stone dovecote in keeping, which stands on one corner of the walled garden. It contains fitted wooden nesting boxes in its upper part. A short distance away at Crowhurst Place, the medieval hall was extended and restored by George Crawley in 1918. At the same time he added several whimsies in the grounds, including the stone dovecote and the gatehouse.

Not all later dovecotes were built in miniature. The large pigeon tower at Rivington in Lancashire was built in 1910 by Robert Atkinson, a pioneer of cinema design, for William Lever, the founder of Lever Brothers. Although in a dilapidated state a decade or so ago, it has recently been well-restored.

Much nearer the present day are two square dovecotes with features in the modern idiom. In 1968 the county architect, A.E.Smith, designed an attractive housing estate complete with a clinic and library at Bicester in Oxfordshire. He used the existing 17th century dovecote as a central focus and embellished it with a transparent acrylic cupola and small windows simulating flight-holes, at the same time transforming it into a functional building. At Wycliffe Hall, County Durham, a rugged stone dovecote which overlooks the lily-pond, was designed by William Whitfield in the 1960s. The ground floor serves as a summerhouse and on each side of the pyramidal roof, seven flight-holes with alighting ledges give access to the pigeon loft above. There are no niches fitted inside, but instead the floor is spread with several inches of sawdust for nesting purposes.

At Longleat House in Wiltshire, Lord Weymouth has had an imaginative dovecote built in his garden within the last decade. It is oval in plan and is supported on six tall columns; beneath the domed roof is a double row of entrance holes. The design was inspired by the cupolas of the house itself.

It is encouraging to realise that today not only are dovecotes still being built, but efforts to create fresh designs continue to fire individual imaginations.

206

CHAPTER XI

# Curiosities

A small number of dovecotes cannot readily be categorized and deserve separate consideration either on account of their scarcity or the singularity of their design.

### Culver Hole and other Caves

Amongst the oddest of all is the primitive but ingeniously adapted cave known as Culver Hole in the coastal cliffs at Port Eynon on the Gower Peninsula in South Wales. The structure of the dovecote comprises a massive sixty-foot high stone wall which seals off the tide-flooded rocky cleft leading to the cave. In this wall there is an entrance doorway at a considerable height above the beach and several round and rectangular openings which admit light and once served as flight-holes. The interior consists of four stages connected by a rough stone stair and the inner face of the wall at all levels is lined with well over 100 L-shaped nesting niches arranged in irregular tiers. The date of its construction is not known. A castle at Port Eynon is mentioned in 1396 but nothing remains and its exact location is obscure. However, a reference of that date to 'the dovecote in the clyve' is believed to relate to Culver Hole. It may, however, have been built as an appendage to the later medieval stronghold of Kulvered Hall or the Salt House in the vicinity, both of which have disappeared. Although many other place names on the coast attest to the Blue Rock pigeon's familiar habit of nesting on cliffs and in caves — as for example at Culvercliff in Bembridge on the Isle of Wight; Culverhole Point at Seaton in Devon; Pigeons Cave on Great Ormes Head at Llandudno in North Wales, and many similarly named in the Hebridean, Orkney and Shetland Islands — there is little evidence that such natural sites were exploited elsewhere apart from one in Scotland at Doo Cave, Lunan Bay in Angus. However, a notable inland adaptation still survives at Carreg Cennen Castle in Dyfed. This great 14th century fortress, of which there are considerable remains, occupies a dramatic hilltop site below which a precipitous escarpment falls away to one side. A cave within this rocky cliff has been sealed by a stone wall which contains pigeon-holes on its inner surface. It is reached from above by a subterranean passage 150 feet long, which traverses the cliff face and has openings to admit both light and birds. There is some doubt as to whether its sole purpose was to serve as a

Interior Elevation

Exterior Elevation

207

dovecote and the date of adaptation is not known. The likelihood of its being contemporary with the castle has been rejected on account of the obvious invitation offered to invaders. In Scotland two other inland caves at Hawthornden Castle, Midlothian, and Sunlaws, Roxburghshire, also contain nest-holes.

There may easily be other adaptations hidden away elsewhere. The advantage of exploiting the birds' natural habitat seems to have been well recognized and was being advocated as recently as 1854 by an expert: 'Those gentlemen who reside in a rocky district might contrive a dovecote by hollowing out a space in the face of a cliff and fashioning the entrance as nearly like a natural cave as possible'.

## Pairs

It is not unknown for two dovecotes to stand within the same demesne, as at Dormston Manor and Huddington Court, in Worcestershire, where they are both timber-framed, but are only roughly similar in appearance. At the large mansion of Ashby St Ledgers, Northamptonshire, its long architectural history dating from Elizabethan times, the two oblong, double, limestone dovecotes are almost identical. Both have twin wooden lanterns, stone gable copings and stone ball finials, but one is slightly smaller than the other; together they contain almost 4,000 nesting boxes. It is not known whether they were built at the same time, but their siting suggests that one was added later, presumably as the household or market need for pigeons increased.

Dovecotes built as one of a pair of buildings are unusual and very few have been preserved. In the farmyard, the granary and dovecote were often neighbours and were sometimes combined in one building, perhaps intentionally, so that the pigeons would grow fat on the gleanings. Occasionally they were built as a matching pair and situated further apart. At Stadhampton in Oxfordshire the octagonal brick dovecote and granary are the only remnants, apart from two gate piers, of Ascott Park which dates from 1666, but was burnt down before its completion. Today they face each other at a distance across an avenue of lime trees in what was once parkland. The dovecote contains more than 600 brick-built nesting places while the almost identical granary, which today differs in having a later thatched roof, has a vaulted cellar, probably intended as an ice-chamber.

Dovecotes specifically built as pairs are also very uncommon. Several Palladian mansions with attached twin pavilions are to be found in this country, but none are known to have been used as paired pigeon houses. The barest resemblance to this arrangement occurs in the north of Scotland on the shores of Sinclair's Bay in Caithness. A pair of large matching lectern dovecotes stand on either side of the ancient Ackergill

Tower. The eastern cote is double and contains nearly 2,000 niches, but its twin has been divided into two storeys and has a fireplace in the upper stage; there are traces of an original partition wall inside, but no sign of nesting boxes. It has been suggested that this cote was left unfinished in the 18th century and the upper part later adapted as a gazebo or prospect room, with wonderful views out to sea. Paired dovecotes of much later date, but built in traditional style are situated further south in Fifeshire. The circular twin towers which stand decoratively on either side of the entrance gate at Balcaskie House were designed in 1911 by the architect, Sir Robert Lorimer.

The earliest of the few surviving pairs in England is to be found at Allington Castle in Kent. These rugged, circular dovecotes are believed to be 12th century in origin and although one has been converted and the other is partially ruined, both contain well-preserved nest-holes. In Hampshire, the later pair of octagonal brick dovecotes connected by a long high wall are, together with the gatehouse, all that remain of the Tudor mansion of Basing House which was stormed and destroyed by Cromwell in 1645; among the prisoners taken was Inigo Jones. One dovecote has a tiled roof with a large wooden dormer pierced by rows of flight-holes. Its circular interior, rounded off to accommodate the potence, is lined with 500 nest-boxes and has occasional brick alighting ledges. The floor has been excavated to a depth of about five feet and several steps descend from

Paired brick dovecotes at
Dogmersfield Park

209

The Wonderful Dovecote,
Castletown

the entrance door to the interior. The second building which has a later
thatched roof has been called a summerhouse and may have been adapted
for the purpose at some time, but there are still undoubted remains of
chalk nests at the base of the walls. As in the other dovecote the floor of this
building is several feet below the threshold, but there is no sign of a
potence. Surviving pairs being so rarely encountered, it seems to be more
than coincidence to find two sets in the same county within ten miles of
each other. At Dogmersfield Park, a short distance away, the pair of square
red brick dovecotes stand on either side of an imposing wrought iron gate.
They have recently been well restored and form a striking ornamental
feature at the entrance to a walled garden.

210

In Ireland a pair of dovecotes with a completely different character is to be found at Castletown, County Kildare. These conical ashlar stone towers with several encircling string courses crown the angles of a large enclosing farm wall, within which stands a much larger barn of similar design. They were all built in the 18th century as eyecatchers for the Palladian mansion and although generally referred to as the Wonderful Barn and the Wonderful Dovecotes, they were also called Babel-like efforts by the locals. Their singular shape is believed to be an imitation of the great Indian rice tower at Patna, but equally possible prototypes are some of the pigeon towers of the Middle East. The Castletown pattern is believed to have been copied at Rathfarnham, near Dublin, where a barn called the Bottle Tower stands beside the conical pigeon tower.

Pairs of dovecotes forming part of a gatehouse or entrance archway are also included in this group. At Hamstall Ridware in Staffordshire, the twin octagonal stone and brick gatehouse towers once housed pigeons and are now the only remains of the Elizabethan manor house of the Fitzherberts. Today the whole structure is in a neglected state and stands forlornly beside modern farm buildings. Each tower contains nesting niches of crude construction and small size, reaching from roof to floor. At Hinton-on-the-Green in Worcestershire, two matching rectangular stone dovecotes, connected by twin arches, feature at the entrance to the manor house. Similarly, the two square supporting columns of the 19th century pedimented gateway at Westwick House in Norfolk were once used to accommodate pigeons. Now demolished, this impressive structure had Gothic Revival doors and windows and was unusual in that the quoins and *voussoirs* of the arch were built of whole flints.

see page 198

Gatehouse dovecotes,
Hinton-on-the-Green

211

*(left)* Breadsall Priory dovecote
*(right)* Brookland Church belltower

## Candle-snuffers Stacked

A print of Breadsall Priory in Derbyshire, dated 1791, illustrates a very strange wooden dovecote whose construction has been likened to four candle-snuffers or four hexagonal truncated cones stacked one above the other. The building, of which no trace remains, tapers upwards and there are spaces between each stage for the birds to come and go. Although the dovecote is probably unique in the records, this singular type of construction can still be seen today in several medieval churches. At St Augustine's church at Brookland in Kent, the fine detached three-staged bell tower is octagonal in plan, while at the church of St Mary at Pembridge in Herefordshire, the bell house is square and comprises four truncated pyramidal storeys. The roof of a vanished square dovecote at Dunston in Norfolk was similar, but consisted of only three stages and terminated in a pointed cupola. Pevsner considers that this style of building is structurally related to the bell houses of Sweden and the stave churches of Norway and,

212

Egyptian Aviary, Tong

as might be expected geographically, was most often used in the eastern counties.

A similar visual effect is reflected fortuitously in the overlapping roofs of the octagonal dovecote and its added loggia for cattle at Swallowfield Park in Berkshire.

## Eccentric Amateurs

The fanciful pyramidal Egyptian aviary at Vauxhall Farm, Tong, in Shropshire, is one of several bizarre outbuildings, including a Gothic cowhouse and a pyramid for pigs, which were conjured up and built on his estate by the wealthy George Durant in the early 19th century. The so-called aviary combines a poultry house on the ground floor with basic accommodation for a few fancy pigeons in the four small upper storeys; no nesting boxes were provided. Built of brick with vitrified quoins, it has alighting ledges below the flight-holes on each stage. Like its companion buildings it once bore several whimsical inscriptions such as 'Scratch before you peck', 'Live and let live', and 'Teach your Granny'!

Another of the many Victorians to take a practical interest in architecture was the High-Churchman, antiquarian, author and hymnologist the Reverend Sabine Baring-Gould. He was both parson and squire at Lewtrenchard in Devon, where he rebuilt the early manor house at the end

213

Semicircular dovecote at Lewtrenchard

of the 19th century. At the same time, he designed the remarkable dovecote in the grounds which is sited as a foil to the ornamental pavilion on the other side of the house. It is semicircular in plan, with two stages, and is built of ashlar stone with granite dressings. An imposing square dormer, which provides access for the birds, is crowned with an arched pediment decorated with obelisk pinnacles. Several other rounded flight-holes in the walls have individual granite ledges supported by granite corbels.

There is no doubt that considerable sparkle has been added to the dovecote scene by these and other flights of imagination.

*CHAPTER XII*

# Confusions and Conversions

**Identification**

Although many dovecotes are hidden away out of sight in parkland or among farm buildings, or even in quite unexpected places, some are visible from roads and footpaths. The more common types are generally recognizable, even from a distance, but others may easily escape identification. Characteristic external features of a dovecote, such as the summit glover or other entrance holes for the birds, may assist, but even these clues can sometimes be misleading. Cupolas and lanterns are often used decoratively on other farm and landscape buildings, while the ventilation holes in barns and the similar 'put-log' holes which sometimes remain after scaffolding beams have been withdrawn, can all confuse the picture. Whether or not these features are present, many dovecotes are not only quite unremarkable but, on cursory inspection, they may be mistaken for a number of other rural buildings. Circular structures of this sort include village lock-ups, toll-houses, decapitated oasthouses and those tower windmills that have lost their sails, a good example of which, now converted into a cottage, is to be seen at Hazelton Grange in Gloucestershire. At Woodchester, in the same county, the stone-built wool-drying tower resembles the tall circular type of early dovecote and is a telling example of mistaken identity. Originally it belonged to one of several woollen mills in the valley south of Stroud and is claimed to be the only complete example left. It has recently undergone conversion into a quaint little house with the attachment alongside of a matching smaller tower.

When viewed from outside, several other buildings, such as well-houses, granaries and the rugged pele-towers of the north bear a close resemblance to square dovecotes, but the most puzzling of all to identify and the most likely ones to be overlooked are those dovecotes constructed as landscape buildings in the 18th century. At this period fewer pigeons were needed for the table and many of the new dovecotes, although still providing housing for some birds, were chiefly built for ornamental and recreational purposes. Together with other features of Georgian landscape architecture, such as banqueting houses, garden pavilions, gazebos and summerhouses, they reflected the newly fashionable appreciation of romantic nature and they comprise an astonishing diversity of design. Their additional use as a retreat for the master of the house is an

*(left)* Wool-drying tower, with addition, at Woodchester
*(right)* The Green House, Alveley

interesting facet, as this piece of advice to a summerhouse builder reveals: 'This small edifice may be made at some remote Angle of your Garden: for the more remote it is, the more private you will be from the frequent disturbances of your Family and Acquaintances'.

### Misconjectures

see page 199

Ambiguities crop up in different forms, often embellished by local legend, as at Bawburgh in Norfolk, where two elegant square ashlar stone buildings, often quoted as being dovecotes, are now incongruously enclosed within adjacent gardens of a modern housing estate. They were built at the end of the 17th century in the grounds of the manor, now demolished. The larger two-storeyed one called the Slipper House, is in a four-gabled design quite foreign to the region and is supposedly the place where pilgrims to the nearby St Walstan's Well deposited their shoes; the smaller building is named the Hermit's House. No valid reason or evidence exists for these designations, nor for the persistent claim that either was built as a dovecote. An early photograph of the larger building shows a row of flight-holes in an adapted upper window which was probably a later change of use and perhaps the source of the popular myth.

Other examples with a passing resemblance to dovecotes have a quite different character. At the Green House, Alveley, in Shropshire a tall square whitewashed building, with a faintly Continental air, stands conspicuously on an angle of the garden wall close to the large farmhouse. It is several-storeyed and now houses poultry on the ground floor. The square perforated panels on each wall, consisting of a honeycomb of clay drainpipes, add a notable decorative feature, but encroach on the interior to the exclusion of any nesting boxes. In spite of this it has been called a dovecote, but it is more likely to have been intended as an ornamental structure concealing some utilitarian activity. The over-generous ventilation suggests some storage or drying function. The hexagonal brick tower with a pyramidal roof on Pepperbox Hill, near Salisbury, Wiltshire, known as Eyre's Folly, offers another feasible confusion, although it contains neither flight-holes nor nest-boxes. The building commands superb views to north and south, but the original upper storey windows and ground-floor arcading have been bricked in. It seems probable that it was built as a prospect tower, but Barbara Jones, writing in the 1950s, must have the last word: 'What Eyre's intention was is difficult to determine: utilitarian or decorative, hunting lodge or belvedere, eyecatcher or folly? Probably a hunting stand'.

see page 199

In these and other equivocal cases, the presence of nesting niches or boxes or traces of them establishes without doubt that a building was used to house pigeons at some time, but it must be remembered that occasionally all sorts of buildings were adapted for the same purpose. In East Anglia, for example, a few of the bases or bucks of disused post windmills were modified in this way; an interesting, probably unique surviving conversion, at Creeting St Mary, was moved from its original site in 1880 before being fitted with nesting boxes. In northern counties and Scotland there are still quite a number of tower windmills which have been adapted for dovecote use. At Haggerston in Northumberland the rubblestone mill was converted in 1828 by the addition of brick nesting holes and a potence. Further south at Spindlestone an 80 foot high, slender threshing mill became known locally as the 'Ducket' with change of use. An early illustration shows circular flight-holes in the upper part and wooden nesting boxes were recorded in 1959. Another unusual 'conversion in reverse' is the brick octagonal garden building with a thatched roof in the grounds of Claremont in Surrey which has recently been adapted to house some white fantails; earlier, it was probably a summerhouse.

Other buildings which have been turned into dovecotes over the centuries include entrance lodges, gatehouses and several church porches

Rockingham Castle

and towers. At Rockingham Castle, Northamptonshire, an 18th century interior conversion utilizes the ground floor of one of the vast semi-circular stone towers of the 13th century gatehouse. Many well-finished ashlar stone nesting places are arranged in two communicating chambers. The only apparent ingress for birds is through an existing arrow-slit.

On the other hand, the total absence of nesting places does not invariably rule out a building's earlier use for pigeons. Wooden boxes were readily removed and in the case of stone or brick construction it was easy to block the holes and remove the ledges, leaving the walls to be rendered if desired. One illustration is to be found at Compton House, Over Compton, Dorset, where the interior of the circular, Ham Hill ashlar stone dovecote has been successfully treated in this way, although careful inspection reveals the mortar of the infilling.

**Adaptations**

As the need for pigeon meat declined, many dovecotes fell into disuse and although a large number of them have crumbled away, some have been converted for other uses. In spite of the fact that their design makes a successful adaptation an expensive challenge, many have already been turned into attractive habitable dwellings. Redundant schools have exemplified this trend in the past and nowadays there is increasing commercial pressure to exploit unusual buildings of all kinds including water-towers, windmills, oasthouses, public conveniences and railway stations.

218

(left) Spacious conversion at Wolverley (see p.112)
(right) Adaptation at the Hall, Bradford-on-Avon

Among those dovecotes that have been converted into dwellings, some have lost their identity more than others. One such example is incorporated in a complex of farm buildings which have been transformed into a smart new housing enclave at Claverton in Avon. The large rectangular dovecote is now totally unrecognizable apart from a deliberately preserved area of exposed pigeon nest-holes in an upstairs bedroom. Was this to satisfy regulations? How long will they remain on view? Other dovecote/cottage conversions are less radical and their character better preserved. The three-storeyed adaptation of an octagonal stone dovecote at Bradford-on-Avon, Wiltshire illustrates the point. The recently altered red brick octagonal cote in Hertfordshire at Little Gaddesden Home Farm, designed originally by an 18th century architect and said to be the finest in the county, and another at Walkern Manor Farm, whose ground floor was originally a granary, might also be considered to be successful examples. Several fine square dovecotes have undergone conversion into desirable properties, such as the substantial four-gabled stone cottage at Barnsley Park in Gloucestershire, the strikingly attractive brick Dutch-gabled building which enhances the environs of a mansion development at Wolverley in Worcestershire and the cosy suburban adaptation, which

see page 200

Allington Castle

see page 200

retains its hipped roof with gablets, at Willington in Bedfordshire.

Generally speaking, the square, rectangular and octagonal types of large dimensions are best suited to domestic conversion, but the adaptation of the circular brick dovecote at Haslingfield in Cambridgeshire and the stone ones of similar shape at Bibury in Gloucestershire and at Allington Castle are notable exceptions.

On an even grander scale is a 1939 conversion of the imposing 16th century stone barn at Shipton Moyne in Gloucestershire, which has created a substantial and unusual country house. On each main elevation of the barn, and rising above it, there is a dominant square tower with a domed roof, surmounted by a rudimentary squat open cupola. Originally, the lower half of each tower formed a typical wagon entrance and the storey above was a pigeon house. Fenestration and the insertion of additional floors has obliterated most of the original pigeon-holes, but several rows remain in the upper roof spaces.

220

Apart from use as human habitation, dovecotes have been adapted for many other purposes over the centuries, of which several instances are still to be found. At Witham Friary in Somerset the rectangular stone monastery dovecote later served as the village parish hall, but is now used as an artist's studio. There are no longer any external clues to its original function.

Very little alteration was needed to turn the tall circular dovecote at Woolavington, Somerset, into a cockpit, but the date of the conversion is not known. This ancient rubblestone structure, which is reputed to have been built in the 14th century on a grange of Downside Abbey, now has a thatched roof, added stone buttresses and two large doorways, one above the other. An early drawing shows that the ground-floor door led to the cock-fighting area while the upper one, reached by an outside wooden staircase, gave access to a small viewing gallery. Today, a central sunken area on the flagstone floor is the only remaining sign of its sporting history. There is no trace of the original nest-holes which were probably blocked and concealed beneath the wall plaster when the building was converted.

see page 200

Shipton Moyne

Stock Gaylard

  There is a more refined conversion at Stock Gaylard in Dorset, where
the pretty circular stone dovecote, with a rainwater head dated 1675 and a
prominent weathervane, was extensively remodelled in 1800 to become a
dairy with added Gothic features; another is at Williamscot House in

Oxfordshire where the lower part of the old dovecote has been made into an orangery with tall, arched windows. At Melbury Sampford in Dorset, a highly ornamental hexagonal stone tower called The Turret stands in excellent order close to Melbury House. It was fitted up as a summerhouse in the 18th century when it was embellished with crocketed pinnacles, a Gothic doorway, plastered walls and an ogee-shaped ribbed ceiling painted with shields of arms. However, parts of the original fabric date from the 16th century, long before the vogue for decorative garden buildings caught on. Might it not therefore have once been a dovecote? What are the possible alternatives? A rather different function is encountered at Melbourne Hall in Derbyshire, where the hexagonal brick cote was altered in the 18th century to become the muniment room. A much more recent adaptation is to be seen at Compton Wynyates in Warwickshire where the octagonal red brick dovecote has been turned into a shop and tearoom for day visitors. The building is hardly changed at all, apart from the boarding up of the lower tiers of pigeon-holes.

Dovecotes have been put to many other changes of use, such as pigsties, garden sheds, game larders, earth closets, peacock houses, smithies, apiaries and cattle shelters. Their temporary role as village lock-up or prison required little structural alteration and has been recorded at Belcombe Court, Compton House and High House, Purfleet, Essex.

Conversion to lock-up at Compton House

223

(*left*) Electricity sub-station at Sherborne Park
(*right*) Simulated dovecote containing water-pump, Lytes Cary

Nearer the present day, very many have been turned into garages, while at Wilcot Manor in Wiltshire, the air-raid shelter conversion in the Second World War of the circular brick and stone dovecote is possibly unique. At Sherborne Park in Gloucestershire the octagonal Cotswold stone pigeon house has recently become an electricity sub-station which serves the modern luxury flats in the adjacent mansion and stableyard.

Finally, there is a small group of buildings masquerading as dovecotes in order to conceal necessary but unattractive facilities. At Lytes Cary Manor in Somerset, the prominently-sited circular structure in typical local dovecote design was built early this century to house water-pumping machinery for the manor. In Herefordshire, two other buildings taking the form of dovecotes, but on a more humble scale, include a 19th century octagonal brick privy at Pembridge and the modern square, brick structure, complete with cupola and mock flight-holes, which houses a fuel-oil tank at Dilwyn.

224

# CHAPTER XIII

# Ruins and Restorations

## Numbers Remaining

A very rough estimate based on several sources including County Schedules of Listed Buildings; Inventories of the Royal Commission for Ancient and Historical Monuments (RCHM); recent surveys conducted by bodies such as the Cornwall Committee for Rescue Archaeology and the Oxfordshire County Council Department of Museum Services; published review articles (see Bibliography); details supplied by individual dovecote enthusiasts and personal data acquired in the field, lead one to suppose that about 1,500 dovecotes are still in existence in England and Wales. This must be an underestimate, because many are unrecognized or overlooked. If each county had keen and knowledgeable chroniclers who would be prepared to seek them out, as has already been done in several districts, the figure would be higher. It is to be hoped that a projected 'Domesday' survey of dovecotes will bring us nearer to the truth (see Appendix A).

Whatever the real figure, our surviving dovecotes represent a fraction of the 26,000 reported in the 17th century. In Herefordshire, for example, Alfred Watkins, the great recorder of dovecotes in that county, reported in 1893 that 55 were lost during several decades around the turn of the century: today, the sum total listed is 61.

In Scotland, a gazetteer recently compiled by the late Dr Grant Peterkin reveals that over 600 doocots are still standing, but apparently more than 300 others have disappeared or become ruinous during this century.

## Dilapidation and Decay

The decay of many dovecotes has been going on ever since the custom of breeding pigeons for food began to decline in the 17th century and since that time thousands have disappeared completely. Once the buildings had become redundant, many deteriorated through neglect while others were demolished for use as building material. Several dovecotes, like their grander relations the country houses, have been deliberately pulled down as recently as the 1950s. An outstanding example at Henham, in Suffolk, designed by James Wyatt, was in pristine order in 1952 but is now completely gone. However, another dovecote attributed to him at Sheffield Park in Sussex has recently been rescued and is to be restored.

Among very ancient stone examples of rugged construction, some have withstood the ravages of time in spite of prolonged neglect, although once the roof has fallen in, disintegration accelerates. For instance, in a graveyard on the Island of Stroma, off the north coast of Scotland, there still stands a roofless, but nevertheless imposing, square grey stone edifice with red sandstone quoins and dressings; built in 1677, this was once a combined burial vault and pigeon house.

Ruins of every degree remain in many districts, ranging from the recognizable to those that have been reduced to a heap of rubble. Others have merely left traces below the surface of the soil. There is considerable documentary evidence to show the sites of lost dovecotes. Medieval examples are commonly associated with religious houses, manor complexes or groups of farm buildings. Recent excavations at Llanthony Priory in South Wales revealed substantial remains of a dovecote sited between the infirmary and the fishponds. During extensive archaeological investigations in 1984 at Dorchester, Dorset, the base of a large circular dovecote, constructed partly of Roman building material, was discovered. A less professional, but still rewarding project, was undertaken in 1975 by a Somerset school whose pupils helped to excavate a dovecote 25 feet in diameter at Butleigh Wood.

The progress of decay is seldom depicted, but occasionally a rough chronicle can be made from chance records. A drawing dated 1844 shows that the medieval stone tower dovecote at Codnor Castle in Derbyshire had already begun to show signs of subsidence due to mining for iron ore beneath it. A photograph taken in 1927 confirmed that the dovecote was still standing although derelict, but deterioration must have continued unchecked because only a heap of stone remained two decades ago. Recently others have collapsed even more rapidly. At Arlingham Court in Gloucestershire, the red brick circular dovecote was intact 30 years ago,

'Listed' building - listed ruins?
Arlingham Court, 1987

226

but today a small segment of the walls and a heap of masonry is all that remains of a listed building. A similar fate overtook the very ancient example at Van, near Caerphilly in South Wales. This ruggedly constructed stone dovecote of the beehive type, similar to those at Manorbier and Angle, was standing in a fair state of preservation until 1947, when it collapsed suddenly after a severe winter.

A ruin of a quite different sort occurs in isolation amongst trees on the north escarpment of the South Downs in Sussex. The large, square flint tower with accommodation for 1,000 pigeons in its middle stage was, until recently, all that remained of the great Tudor house of Michelgrove which was demolished in the 19th century. The original two-storeyed dovecote was later embellished by a third storey housing a turret clock with four dials, subsequently removed and installed above Steyning Town Hall. A photograph taken a couple of decades ago shows the tower already crumbling and today only a pile of rubble remains. Several neglected

Michelgrove clock tower and dovecote before collapse

227

Roofless ruin at Piddletrenthide

dovecotes in which decay is less advanced still survive as spectacular ruins. Some are roofless and have vegetation sprouting from the walls; others are engulfed by undergrowth both inside and out. A few are even picturesque, particularly those designed in neo-Gothic style as at Sulham in Berkshire, Davenport in Worcestershire, Piddletrenthide in Dorset and Gatton Bottom in Surrey. Despite this altogether sad story, many of these roofless ruins present a strangely romantic view of their interiors.

228

More dilapidation:
*(top)* Stoke-sub-Hamdon;
*(bottom left)* Burton Court;
*(bottom right)* Clattercote

229

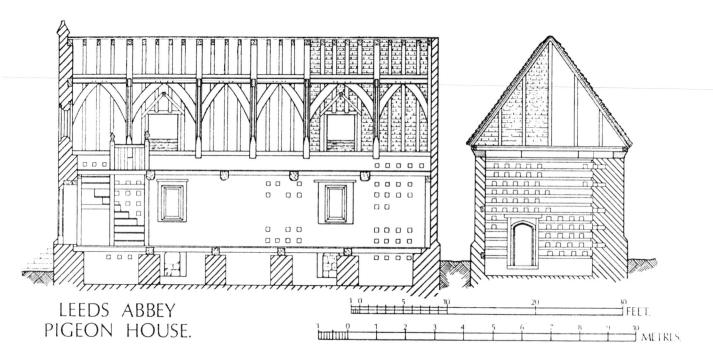

LEEDS ABBEY
PIGEON HOUSE.

1 0     5        10              20                  40
⊢┼┼┼┼┼┼┼┼┼┼┼┼┼┼┼┼┼┼┼┼┼┼┼┼┼┤ FEET.

1      0    1    2    3    4    5    6    7    8    9    10
⊢┼┼┼┼┤ METRES.

Probable structure of ruined
dovecote at Leeds Abbey Farm

A few dovecote ruins conceal an unexpectedly interesting history, particularly when there have been several structural alterations over the centuries. This is epitomised by the remains of two adjacent buildings at Leeds Abbey Farm in Kent, whose chronology has recently been painstakingly unravelled. They stand on the site of an Augustinian priory founded in the 12th century. The original square medieval pigeon house was greatly extended lengthwise at the end of the 16th century to make one continuous building containing 1,000 nests. This rectangular dovecote, with a corbelled gable, a cupola and dormer windows, is clearly shown in a print of 1720 by Thomas Badeslade. In 1777, Capability Brown gave the dovecote a sham façade to convey the distant impression of a chapel as part of his landscaping of the abbey grounds. To this end, two windows with fashionable Gibbs surrounds were inserted and an existing window was similarly treated. Subsequently the pigeon house was divided into two at the point of the original extension. Floors and a staircase were installed in the larger building and practically every nest-hole was filled in with bricks, the ledges removed and all the walls coated with clay rendering. Later vicarious uses of the building have finally obscured its original identity.

The building of mock ruins as eyecatchers in the landscape flourished at the end of the 18th century. One of the few, possibly the only dovecote to be incorporated in such an edifice, still stands at Bavington Hall in

230

Northumberland. This combined dovecote and greyhound coursing pavilion stands alone in open countryside and has been used in living memory for keeping pigeons and coursing dogs. This sport, like pigeon shooting, was popular in the 19th century.

## Conservation

There can be little doubt that dovecotes are an intriguing and irreplaceable part of our heritage. Current enthusiasm for conservation together with the statutory listing of buildings of architectural and historical importance, recently expanded to include vernacular architecture, should ensure preservation of remaining worthwhile examples, but in practice some still seem to slip through the net. Nowadays, in addition to the threats of neglect, decay and destruction, there is increasing pressure in rural areas to adapt dovecotes, together with other redundant farm buildings, for alternative uses. The current agricultural depression has emphasized the need to capitalize on their development in various ways, including conversion into weekend cottages and as premises for light industry. This policy receives encouragement from above, but may create a conflict for the planning authorities. It is widely believed that restrictions on some Listed Buildings are being relaxed and certainly a few dovecotes of merit have recently been turned into domestic dwellings. Such opportunities for development are widely advertised, as in the case of the following Grade II listed dovecote: 'Carefully converted into an open-plan house retaining many original features, up to four bedrooms and a self-contained annexe'. Surely, the line must be drawn somewhere or else any sizeable listed dovecote will qualify for this sort of cavalier treatment.

It can be argued that conversion is a method of conservation and, at least, it preserves the bare fabric of the building, but is it the best means? This trend is by now probably irreversible, but in its wake comes a pressing need to ensure that dovecotes are carefully recorded before they become altered out of all recognition.

In spite of disheartening tales, there is room for some optimism. Many dovecotes in private hands have been carefully maintained over the years and this custodianship mostly continues, often against the odds. Bodies such as the National Trust; the Department of the Environment; English Heritage; the Historic Buildings Council; the Society for the Preservation of Ancient Buildings; Parish Councils; Local Authorities and more recently the Manpower Services Commission, are now playing an important role in conservation. A newer and increasingly active group in this field comprises local amenity societies and building preservation trusts whose members have risen voluntarily to the challenge in many parts of the country. Their interest and enthusiasm have provided the mainspring

231

for many worthwhile projects and several dovecotes have already been salvaged under their auspices.

## Museums

Examples of present restoration work are too numerous to quote individually, but some noteworthy efforts have been championed by museums. The Angus Historical Society's adaptation of the large two-chambered doocot at Finavon in Scotland has created a museum devoted to the history of pigeon farming in one half and a stocked dovecote visible through a glass partition in the other. In Nottinghamshire, part of the stable block at Wollaton Park has been utilized as an industrial museum and the adjacent restored dovecote is to be incorporated into the scheme. A different slant at Bleasby, also in Nottinghamshire, concentrates on the idea of farm-based tourism. The manor farm dovecote has been restored and houses an exhibition of old farm implements, while the adjoining barn and stable complex have been turned into a leisure area including a children's farm complete with young animals. A similar arrangement has been exploited at Cricket St Thomas.

Other enterprising rescue operations of a different kind have been launched recently by two open-air museums. The Avoncroft Museum of Buildings at Bromsgrove has dismantled a derelict dovecote at Haselour Hall in Staffordshire and restored and re-erected it on their site. They have also undertaken other restorations *in situ* at Hill Croome near Upton-upon-Severn and at Moat Farm, Dormston, both in Worcestershire. In Sussex a crumbling flint-built dovecote from a farm in the Cuckmere valley has recently been taken down stone by stone and transported to the Weald and Downland Open Air Museum at Singleton, where it will ultimately be restored and reassembled.

All this work is highly commendable, but its continuation must depend to a great extent on the vigilance and cooperation of an interested public.

*Old barns become as much sought after as toll houses, oast houses and windmills all of which are listed to prevent our past from being consigned to the skip. It seems to me a great pity we slept on it for so long and woke up so late.* (Ian Niall, 1987)

232

## APPENDIX A

# Data Form for Field Studies

The circumstances leading to the issue by the Ancient Monuments Society of the following questionary about dovecotes in 1956 are not clear.

Apparently, it was distributed widely by post and resulted in a complete or partial response from many hundreds of tenants and owners. The task of collating and classifying the information thus obtained proved too daunting at the time and it was only partially explored.

The project is fully acknowledged and commented upon in an unpublished manuscript (also held by the AMS) by the late Reginald Harrison, who extracted a great deal of information from these records in the early 1970s which he was able to incorporate and embellish in his own work.

Harrison suggested that the AMS record form was unnecessarily detailed and too cumbersome for practical field work and so derived his own simplified version which was confined to site; materials used; shape; roof shape and cover; wall thickness; approximate date; and number of nest-holes.

The original form is reprinted here in the hope that it will provide an adaptable framework for others interested in pursuing local or regional surveys. The topic itself offers good potential project material for schools and adult further education studies, which could usefully contribute to the overall picture.

# ANCIENT MONUMENTS SOCIETY

**Information on Dovecote at**.............................................................

**Map Reference**.....................

## GENERAL.

1. Name and address of owner.  (1.).................................................................
.................................................................
.................................................................

2. Name and address of tenant, if the cote is let separately, or let with another property.  (2.).................................................................
.................................................................
.................................................................

3. Proximity of cote to main building, or is cote part of another building.  (3.).................................................................
.................................................................

4. Position of cote, *i.e.*, ground level, a hill, or mound of high ground, etc.  (4.).................................................................
.................................................................

## STRUCTURE.

5. Type of cote, *i.e.*, ecclesiastical, manorial, etc.  (5.).................................................................
.................................................................

6. Of what material is the cote constructed, *i.e.*, stone, brick, timber, etc., or combination of materials.  (6.).................................................................
.................................................................
.................................................................

7. Shape of cote, *i.e.*, square, octagonal, circular, rectangular, etc.  (7.).................................................................
.................................................................

8. Type of floor to the cote, *i.e.*, stone, brick, puddled clay, tile, etc.  (8.).................................................................
.................................................................

9. Shape of roof, *i.e.*, hipped, gabled, conical, etc.  (9.).................................................................
.................................................................

10. Roof covering, *i.e.*, stone flags, slates, red tile, grey slate, wood shingles, etc.  (10.).................................................................
.................................................................
.................................................................

11. Termination and finial of roof, *i.e.*, gabled, louvred; also state whether surmounted by weather-vane, etc.  (11.).................................................................
.................................................................
.................................................................

234

12. External measurements of building. (12.)................................................................................................
.........................................................................................................

13. Internal measurements or thickness of walls. (13.)................................................................................................
.........................................................................................................

14. Does the building bear a date, or any incised inscription, coat of arms, etc.; if so, in what form. (14.)................................................................................................
.........................................................................................................
.........................................................................................................

15. Approximate date of construction. (15.)................................................................................................

16. Is the work original or much restored. (16.)................................................................................................

17. Is the cote in good repair or ruinous. (17.)................................................................................................

18. Is the building in any danger of demolition. (18.)................................................................................................
.........................................................................................................

19. If the cote is ruinous, how much of the .structure survives. (19.)................................................................................................
.........................................................................................................

20. Is the building scheduled as an Ancient Monument. (20.)................................................................................................
.........................................................................................................

21. Is the building listed under the Town and Country Planning Acts as " a building of outstanding architectural or historic interest." (21.)................................................................................................
.........................................................................................................
.........................................................................................................
.........................................................................................................

## NESTING ARRANGEMENTS.

22. The number of tiers of nests. (22.)................................................................................................

23. The number of nests in each tier. (23.)................................................................................................

24. What are the nesting boxes made of, *i.e.*, brick, stone, wood, tile, or puddled clay. (24.)................................................................................................
.........................................................................................................
.........................................................................................................

25. Is the cote still used by pigeons. (25.)................................................................................................

26. Are the nests ' L ' shaped. (26.)................................................................................................

27. Approximate measurements of nest, *i.e.*, 18″ deep. (27.)................................................................................................
.........................................................................................................

28. Are nests grouped on all sides of cote. (28.)................................................................................................
.........................................................................................................

29. Is there an alighting board or ledge for pigeons; if so, how many tiers and nests to each alighting board. (29.)................................................................................................
.........................................................................................................
.........................................................................................................

30. Are the nests reached by ladder or potence. (30.)............................................................................

31. Is there an alighting board to potence. (31.)............................................................................

32. How do the birds enter the cote, *i.e.*, by roof louvre entrance, or holes cut in gable end, etc. (32.)............................................................................

33. Are there doors and windows to the cote; if so, where are they situated, and at what level. (33.)............................................................................

34. Is there any protection revealed on the structure to prevent vermin entering the cote. (34.)............................................................................

## MISCELLANEOUS PARTICULARS.

35. By what name is the building commonly known, *i.e.*, Pigeon house, Pigeon tower, duffus, dove house, dovecote, etc. (35.)............................................................................

36. Any feature peculiar to this dovecote. (36.)............................................................................

37. Has the dovecote to your knowledge been described in any printed publication. If so, please give precise reference. (37.)............................................................................

38. Are current photographs and / or drawings available. (38.)............................................................................

39. Is there a plan available. (39.)............................................................................

40. Is there any story or legend associated with the dovecote(s). (40.)............................................................................

# *APPENDIX B*

# Some Accessible Sites

*It must be stressed that a number of the dovecotes illustrated in this book, and others not listed here, lie on strictly private land far from any path or road and if a visit should be desired, the courtesy of a written request to the owner or occupier must be the rule.*

However, there are certainly very many dovecotes not mentioned here that await an innocent sighting!

As a starting point, the following is a list of National Trust properties, open to the public, which sport a dovecote. In some cases the interiors may be viewed:

Antony House, Torpoint, Cornwall
Benthall Hall, Broseley, Shropshire
Blaise Hamlet, Westbury-on-Trym, Bristol, Avon
Bruton, Somerset
Cliveden, Taplow, Buckinghamshire
Cotehele House, St Dominick, nr Saltash, Cornwall
Erddig, nr Wrexham, Clwyd
Felbrigg Hall, Norwich, Norfolk
Gunby Hall, nr Spilsby, Lincolnshire
Hawford Dovecote, Hereford & Worcester
Kinwarton Dovecote, Warwickshire
Nymans Garden, Handcross, West Sussex
Snowshill Manor, nr Broadway, Gloucestershire
Stoke-sub-Hamdon Priory, nr Montacute, Somerset
Wichenford Dovecote, Hereford & Worcester
Willington Dovecote & Stables, Willington, Bedfordshire

The following is a selective list of locations and properties at which several typical dovecotes may be seen without difficulty or fear of trespass; many are illustrated within the text:

(EH) - English Heritage
(G) - Grounds open to the public at certain times of the year.

Abington Park, Northamptonshire
Avebury Museum & Great Barn, Wiltshire (G)
Athelhampton, Dorset

237

Avoncroft Museum of Buildings, Bromsgrove, Hereford & Worcester
Basing House, Old Basing, Hampshire (G)
Belcombe Court, Bradford-on-Avon, Wiltshire (G)
Blackford House Farm, nr Luccombe, Somerset
Blockley, Gloucestershire
Chastleton House, Oxfordshire
Chicheley Hall, Buckinghamshire (G)
Conisborough Castle, Yorkshire (EH)
Dunster, Somerset
Eardisland, Hereford & Worcester
Hodnet Hall Gardens, Shropshire (G)
Hangleton Manor Hotel, nr Brighton, East Sussex (G)
Low Middleton Hall, Middleton St George, County Durham
Luntley Court, Hereford & Worcester
Manorbier Castle, Dyfed
Minster Lovell Hall & Dovecote, Oxfordshire (EH)
Motcombe Gardens, Eastbourne, East Sussex
Netheravon, Wiltshire (EH)
Newtimber Place, Newtimber, West Sussex (G)
Norton-sub-Hamdon, Somerset
Painswick House & Rococo Garden, Painswick, Gloucestershire (G)
Parham Park Gardens, Parham, West Sussex (G)
Patcham, nr Brighton, East Sussex
Penmon Priory, Anglesey (CADW)
Rockingham Castle, Northamptonshire (G)
Rousham House, Rousham, Oxfordshire (G)
Sulham, nr Reading, Berkshire
Shapwick House Hotel, Shapwick, Somerset
Whitehall, Shrewsbury, Shropshire
White Hart, Wytham, Oxfordshire
Witton Castle, Witton-le-Wear, County Durham (G)

Particular attention should be drawn to open-air museums such as the Avoncroft Museum of Buildings mentioned here as having a beautifully restored dovecote and the Weald and Downland Museum at Singleton, near Chichester, which has a dovecote awaiting re-erection.

238

# Acknowledgements

It is a pity that the acknowledgement pages of any book are not more seriously read, for they frequently mean more than the observance of a convention. The background information upon which much of this account has been based could not have been obtained without the help of many people. We are thankful to them all.

Several national institutions, which tend to be taken very much for granted, have provided invaluable reference material and we are indebted to the British Library, the British Museum, the National Monuments Record, the British Architectural Library, the National Trust and the Sir John Soane's Museum Library. In addition, several county archivists and members of local archaeological and preservation societies have contributed usefully.

We are particularly grateful to the majority of planning authorities whose positive help and cooperation has more than made up for the few in which it was lacking for one reason or another and we must also thank the many librarians who have rendered assistance; in particular Mrs M. Joyce and staff at the Bath Reference Library.

Personal thanks are due to Leslie Almond, Dr R. G. Anderson, J. Bevington, T. Buxbaum, Michael Seago, John Severn, Capt. Peter Tatton-Brown, and Alan Whitworth for their interest; also to Matthew Saunders of the Ancient Monuments Society for providing access to the unpublished manuscript of the late Reginald Harrison. It would be impossible to mention all those others who have been to considerable lengths to lend their support, but it is hoped that they will recognize their contribution.

Special appreciation must be expressed to the many patient landowners who have provided so much interesting information and, often at some inconvenience, have graciously conducted us or allowed us to tramp about their property.

Our friend and colleague, Keith Duguid, has been of inestimable help in seeing us through numerous photographic vicissitudes and we are greatly in his debt.

Finally, thanks are due to our publishers, Tim Graham and Alan Summers, whose enthusiasm and meticulous attention to each stage of the production of this book must not go unremarked.

# Picture Credits

Although most of the photographs have been produced by the authors, the following individual credits are due for pictures on the pages mentioned:

Leonard Beard, 199 (top), 200 (top left)
Elizabeth Beaton (and artists Bruce Walker & Mike Brown), 84 (margin), 112 (top margin)
Graham Beaumont, 97 (right), 192 (right)
Elizabeth Beazley, 42
Keith and Susan Bennett, 94 (top), 119 (top left)
Oliver Bott, Conservation Officer, Chester County Planning Department, 195 (bottom)
Dr Leslie Bowcock, 195 (top right)
British Architectural Library, RIBA, London, 184, 185
British Library, 10, 12, 18, 26, 27, 43, 74, 80, 146, 174, 189, 192 (left), 202, 212 (left)
The Trustees of the British Museum, 14
Nesta Caiger, 228
Alistair Campbell of Airds, the Younger, 181
Director of Architecture, Planning and Estates, Clwyd County Council, 130 (centre)
Devon County Council, 77 (top left)
Eastbourne Civic Society, D. Forrester, 88
Edinburgh University Press, 180
W. Green, Richmondshire District Council Planning Department, 177 (right)
Hammersmith & Fulham Archives, 32
Adrian Hansell, 65, 77 (bottom left), 214
The late Reg Harrison, 87 (margin), 101, 217
Hurlingham Club, 33
The Irish Architectural Archive, Dublin, 210
R.H. Longbridge and Domestic Buildings Research Group (Surrey), 97 (margin)
Leicestershire Museums, Art Galleries & Record Services, 187 (top)
Jeremy Lowe, 44 (top)
Peter Messenger, 133
Mitchell Beazley, 168 (bottom margin)
The National Gallery, 169
National Trust (Northern Ireland), 99
National Trust (Severn Region), 128
Raymond Phillips, 200 (top right, bottom right)
E.G. Price, 103 (margin)
Racing Pigeon Pictorial, 20
RCHAM (Scotland), 84, 181
RCHM (England), 51 (left), 123, 149 (bottom), 177 (top), 182, 190
RCHM (Wales), 62, 75, 108, 149, (top), 172, 203, 207
Rosemary Robertson, 77 (bottom right)
Viscount Scarsdale, 186
Michael Shepherd, 155
Sir John Soane's Museum Library, 187 (bottom), 188
Garry Swann, 66 (top)
Victoria Art Gallery & Bath City Council, 179 (left)
West Pennine Moors Area Management Committee, 206
Roger White, 179 (right)
Neil Wishart, 46

Barbara Frears was specially commissioned to execute many of the marginal sketches and the sectional drawing on p.48 which together have made such a notable contribution to the book.

# Bibliography and Sources

The following entries relate chiefly to England & Wales, but include some references to Scottish and French publications.

## Books

Anon. (1740), *The Dovecote, or the Art of Breeding Pigeons,* Joseph Davidson at the Angel in Poultry, London.

Aldrovandi, Ulisse (1599), *Ornithologiae,* Lib. XV (Pt.II), 353-461, Bologna.

Aristotle, trans. Creswell, R. (1862), *The History of Animals,* Henry G. Bohn, London.

Ayrton, Elizabeth (1977), *The Cookery of England,* Penguin Books, Harmondsworth.

Baker, P.S. (1933), 'Some Famous War Pigeons' in *Animal War Heroes,* A. & C. Black, London.

Beaton, Elizabeth (1978), *The Doocots of Moray,* The Moray Field Club.
    (1980), *The Doocots of Caithness,* The Scottish Vernacular Buildings Working Group, Dundee.

Beazley, E & Harveson, M. (1982), 'Pigeon Towers' in *Living with the Desert,* Aris & Phillips, Warminster.

Blomfield, Reginald (1892), *The Formal Garden in England,* reprinted 1985, Macmillan, London.

Bogaerts, Felix (1847), *Histoire Civile et Religieuse de la Colombe,* Anvers, France.

Brunskill, R.W. (1982), *Traditional Farm Buildings of Britain,* Victor Gollancz, London.

Buffon, Comte de (Le Clerc) (1793), *Natural History of Birds,* vol. ii, Strahan & Cadell, London.

Buxbaum, T. (1987), Scottish Doocots, Shire Publications, (Album No. 190), Aylesbury.

Cato the Censor, trans. Brehaut (1933), *On Farming,* Columbia University Press, New York.

Chamberlain, E. (1907), *The Homing Pigeon,* The Homing Pigeon Publishing Co., Manchester.

*Chambers Encyclopaedia* (1901), "Carrier Pigeon", vol. viii, William & Robert Chambers, London & Edinburgh.

Chapman, Vera (1977), 'On the Wing' in *Rural Durham,* Durham County Council, Durham.

Clarke, Gillian (1987), *Prior Park — A Compleat Landscape,* Millstream Books, Bath.

Columella, L.J.M., trans. Ash, H.B. (1941), *De Re Rustica,* William Heinemann, London.

Cooke, A.O. (1920), *A Book of Dovecotes,* T.N. Foulis, London.

Cran, Marion (1934), *The Squabbling Garden,* Herbert Jenkins, London.
    (1935), *Making the Dovecote Pay,* Herbert Jenkins, London.

Darby, W.J., Ghalioungi, P. & Grivetti, L. (1977), *Food: The Gift of Osiris,* Academic Press, London.

Darwin, Charles (1885), *The Variation of Animals & Plants under Domestication,* John Murray, London.

Delamer, E.S. (1854), *Pigeons and Rabbits,* Routledge, London.

Dorling, T. (1953), *History of the Hurlingham Club,* The Hurlingham Club, London.

Fowler, Peter (1983), *Farms in England,* figs, 90-95, HMSO, London.

Girton, Daniel (1785), *The Complete Pigeon Fancyer,* Alexander Hogg, London.

Goodwin, D. (1983), *Pigeons and Doves of the World,* British Museum, London.

Grigson, Geoffrey (1978), *The Goddess of Love,* Quartet Books, London.

Hall, R. & Z. (1972), *A Bibliography on Vernacular Architecture,* David & Charles, Newton Abbot, Devon.

Hansell, P & J. (1988), *Dovecotes,* Shire Publications, Album No. 213, Aylesbury.

Harting, J.E. (1871), *The Ornithology of Shakespeare,* H. Cox, London.

Harvey, C.N. (1970), *A History of Farm Buildings in England and Wales,* David & Charles, Newton Abbot, Devon.

Henderson, C.G. (1935), 'Cornish Culverhouses' in *Essays in Cornish History,* Clarendon Press, Oxford.

Heresbachius Conradius (1577), *Foure Bookes of Husbandry*, Richard Watkins, London.

Houlihan, P.F. (1986), *The Birds of Ancient Egypt*, Aris & Phillips, Warminster.

Hunt, Peter (1964), 'Dovecotes and Columbaria' in *The Shell Gardens Book*, Phoenix House, London.

Ingersoll, E. (1923), *Birds in Legend, Fable & Folklore*, Longman, London.

Jeevar, Peter (1953), *Dovecotes of Cambridgeshire*, Oleander Press, Cambridge.

Jones, Barbara (1974), *Follies and Grottoes*, Constable, London.

Kinmonth, P. & Cartwright, R. (1979), *Mr Potter's Pigeon*, Hutchinson, London.

Lambton, Lucinda (1985), *Beastly Buildings*, Jonathan Cape, London.

Leron-Lesur, P. (1986), *Colombiers et Pigeonniers en France*, Editions Ch. Massin, Paris.

Levi, Wendell M. (1981), *The Pigeon*, Levi Publishing Co., Sumter, USA.

Lindsay, I.G. & Cosh, Mary (1973), *Inveraray and the Dukes of Argyll*, Edinburgh University Press, Edinburgh.

Lodge, Barton (ed.1873), *Palladius on Husbondrie*, from 1420 manuscript in Colchester Castle, Early English Text Society, London.

Lucas, Revd J. (1886), *The Pleasures of a Pigeon Fancier*, Sampson Low, London.

Lumley, W.F. (1895), *Fulton's Book of Pigeons*, Cassell, London.

Markham, G. (1613), *The English Husbandman*, J. Browne, London.

Mason, I.L. (1984), *Evolution of Domesticated Animals*, Longman, London.

Messent, C.J.W. (1928), *Dovecotes and Farm Buildings in the Old Cottages and Farm-houses of Norfolk*, H.W. Hunt, Norwich.

Moore, John (1735), *Columbarium or the Pigeon House — being an Introduction to a Natural History of Tame Pigeons*, J. Wilford, London.

Morier, James (1812), *A Journey through Persia, Armenia and Asia Minor*, Longman, London.

Nalder, R.F.H. (1953). 'Signal Despatch and Pigeons' in *The History of the British Army Signals in World War II*, Royal Signals Institution, London.

Ordish, G. & Binder, Pearl (1967), *People and Pigeons*, Dennis Dobson, London.

Osman A.H. (1919), *Pigeons in the Great War*, Racing Pigeon Publishing Co., London.

Osman, W.H. (1946), *Pigeons in World War II*, Racing Pigeon Publishing Co., London.

Palladio, Andrea, ed. Leoni, Giacomo (1715, 1720), *The Architecture of Andrea Palladio*, London.

Penhallurick, R.D. (1978), 'The Dovecotes of Cornwall' in *Birds of Cornwall and the Isles of Scilly*, Headland Publications, Penzance.

Peterkin, G.A.G. (1980), *Scottish Dovecotes*, William Culross, Coupar Angus, Scotland.

Pevsner, N. (several editions 1951-1974), *Buildings of England* (multiple volumes by county), Penguin Books, Harmondsworth.

Pliny, trans. Rackman, H. (1940), *Natural History*, William Heinemann, London.

Potter, Beatrix (1955), *The Tale of the Faithful Dove*, Frederick Warne, London.

Pridham, J.C. (1974), *Dove and Pigeon Cotes in Worcestershire*, County Planning Dept., Worcester.

Ray, J. (1678), *The Ornithology of F. Willughby*, London.

RCAHM (Wales) (1981), *Glamorgan: The Greater Houses*, vol.iv, HMSO, London.

RCHM (England), *Inventory of Architectural Monuments — Huntingdonshire* (1926), *West Dorset* (1952), *Dorset* (1970), *Northamptonshire* (1981/1984),

Robertson, Rosemary & Gilbert, G. (1979), *Some Aspects of the Domestic Archaeology of Cornwall*, Institute of Cornish Studies, Redruth.

Robinson, J.M. (1983), *Georgian Model Farms*, Clarendon Press, Oxford.

Salmon, W. (1693), *Seplasium, or the English Physician*, London.

Selby, P.J. (1835), 'The Natural History of Pigeons' in *Naturalist's Library*, vol. xix, Lizars, Edinburgh.

Serres, Olivier de (1600). *Le Théâtre d'Agriculture et Mesnage des Champs*, Paris.

Severn, J.A. (1986), *Dovecotes of Nottinghamshire*, Cromwell Press, Newark.

Simms, Eric (1979), *The Public Life of the Street Pigeon*, Hutchinson, London.

Smith, Donald (1931), *Pigeon Cotes and Dove Houses of Essex*, Simpkin Marshall, London.

*Sportsman's Dictionary, The* (1725), entries under 'Pigeons' & 'Pigeon Houses', Fielding & Walker, London.

Stainburn, I.R. (1979), *A Survey of Dovecotes in the Old County of Herefordshire*, County Planning Department, Worcester.

242

Storey, Graham (1951), *Reuters' Century*, Max Parrish, London.

Tegetmeier, W.B. (1868), *Pigeons: their Structure, Varieties, Habits and Management*, Routledge, London.

Thomas, Michael (1980), *Dovecotes*, National Trust (Severn Region) & Avoncroft Museum of Buildings, Bromsgrove.

Tusser, Thomas (1580/1878 edition), *Five Hundred Pointes of Good Husbandrie*, English Dialect Society, London.

Varro, M.T., trans. Best, L.S. (1912), *De Re Rustica*, Bell, London.

Waterton, C. (1857), *Essays on Natural History*, Longman Green, London.

Watts, Kathleen (1980), *Colombiers et Pigeonniers*, Editions CLD, France.

Whitaker, J. (1927), *A Descriptive List of Medieval Dovecotes in Nottinghamshire*, Mansfield Reporter, Nottingham.

Wiliam, E. (1982), *Traditional Farm Buildings in Wales (1550-1900)*, National Museum of Wales, Cardiff.

Willis, R. (1886), *The Architectural History of the University of Cambridge*, Cambridge University Press, Cambridge.

Wilson, Anne C. (1973), *Food and Drink in England*, Penguin Books, Harmondsworth.

Zeuner, F.E. (1963), *A History of Domesticated Animals*, Hutchinson, London.

# Articles

Alexander, P. (1936), 'Ancient Dovecotes', *Cheshire Life* (March), 18-21.

Andrews, H.C. (1907), 'Dovecotes', *East Herts. Archaelog. Soc.* 3 (Pt.III), 297-303.

Armstrong, C.M.C. (1943), 'Ancient Dovecotes', *Warwickshire Journal*, 1, No.20.

Beacham, M. (1989). 'A Gazetteer of English Dovecotes', *Trans. of Ancient Monuments Society*, New Series, 33 (in press).

Beaumont, G. (1975), 'Dovecotes', *Heritage — The Nottinghamshire Newsletter*, (Spring), 6-8.

Berkeley, M. (1905/6), 'The Dovecotes of Worcestershire', *Assoc. of Architects Soc.*, 333-349.

Bertram, Colin & Mark (1969), 'Pigeon Towers of Isfahan', *Geographical Magazine*, 41, 516.

Buncombe, G.E. (1960), 'Dovehouses and the 'Duffus' in Essex', *Essex Countryside*, 8, 62-63.

Buxbaum, T. (1985), 'A Taste for Pigeons', *Out of Town*, (June), 20-22.

Caiger, John E.L. (1974), 'Two Kent Pigeon Houses', *Archaeologica Cantiana*, 89, 33-39.

Chambers, Chas. D. (1921), 'Romano-British Dovecotes', *Society for the Promotion of Roman Studies*, 10,5131.

Cheetham, F.H. (1924), 'Notes on North Meols', *Hist. Soc. of Lancs. & Cheshire*, 1, 76, 80-86.

Copeland, G.W. (1937), 'Devon Dovecotes', *Reports & Trans. Devonshire Assoc.*, 69, 391-401.

David-Roy, Marguerite (1964), 'Colombiers et Pigeonniers', *Medecine de France*, 155, 21-31.

Dickens, C. (1850), 'Winged Telegraphs', *Household Words*, 1, 19, 454-456.

Evans, D.H. et al (1983/4), 'Further Excavations and Fieldwork at Llanthony Priory', *Proc. Monmouth Antiquarian Assoc.*, 5, Pts. 1&2, 44-47.

Farmer, Peter G. (1981), 'A Dovecote at Brompton', *The Dalesman*, March, 985-986.

Fergusson, R.S. (1887/8), 'Pigeon Houses in Cumberland', *Cumberland & Westmoreland Antiq. & Archaeolog. Soc.*, 9, 412-434.

(1887), 'Culverhouses', *Archaeological Journal*, 64, 105-116.

Gardner, Iltyd (1910), 'A Semi-subterranean Columbarium, Llanthony', *Cambrian Archaeolog. Assoc.* 9, 157-160.

Grange, Hope (1937), 'Dovecotes in Somerset', *Somerset Yearbook*, 81.

Grice, E. (1979), 'Dovecotes, The Lord's 'Larder'', *The Period Home*, 1, 4, 14-19.

Hansell, Jean (1986), 'Dovecotes', *Period Home*, 7, Jan, 47-53, Feb, 25-28.

(1986), 'Living In', *Heritage — the British Review*, 8, Feb/Mar, 64-66.

Hanson, Elisha (1926), 'Man's Feathered Friend of Longest Standing', *National Geographic Magazine*, 19, 63-110.

Horne, E (1919/23), 'Manorial Dovecotes and Fishponds', *Somerset Archaeolog. & Nat. Hist. Soc.* (Bath & Dist. Branch), 160-165.

Hornell, J. (1947), 'Egyptian and Medieval Pigeon Houses', *Antiquity*, 21, 182-185.

Hutton, Barbara (1964), 'Interesting Dovecots in Hertfordshire', *Herts. Countryside*, 19, 164-165.

*Illustrated London News* (1844), 'Nooks and Corners of Old England — Ancient Dovecots', 4/5, 36.

James, H.A. (1968) 'Kent Dovecotes and Pigeon Houses', *Kent Life*, August, 46-47.

Jerram-Burrows, L.E. (1960), 'Rochford's Unique Dovecote', *Essex Countryside*, 8, 244.

Law, William (1914/16), 'Our Ancient Dovecotes', *Brighton & Hove Archaeologist*, 1/3, 128-142.
    (1932), 'Some Ancient Sussex Dovecotes', *Sussex County Magazine*, 6, 284-293.
    (1932), 'Old Dovecotes in the Cuckmere Valley', *Sussex County Magazine*, 6, 635-639.
    (1934), 'Some Ancient Sussex Dovecotes', *Sussex County Magazine*, 8, 621.

Lea, Raymond (1981), 'A Look at Local Dovecotes', *Berks. & Bucks. Countryside*, Sept, 20-21.

Lloyd, G. (1965/6), 'Flintshire Dovecotes', *Jnl. Flint. Hist. Soc.*, 22, 78-82.

Mason, Jim (1980), 'Pigeons — A Welcome Addition to the Diet of any Household', *Coast & Country*, 9, 3, 12-13.

Mowat, G. (1898), 'Early Pigeon Houses in St Albans and Hertfordshire', *Architect. & Archaeolog. Soc.*, 2, 28-33.

Palmer, Joyce & M. (1982), 'Northamptonshire Dovecotes', *Bedfordshire Life*, June, 39.

Pearse, W.T. (1944), 'More notes on Northamptonshire Dovecotes', *Northants. Architect. Soc.*, 50, 8.

Price, E.G. (1980), 'Survivals of the Medieval Monastic Estate of Frocester', *Trans. Bristol & Glos. Archaeological Soc.* 98, 73-88.

Price, Harriet (1928), 'Dovecotes of the South Downs', *Sussex County Magazine*, 2, 395-396.

Randall, D. & J. (1987), 'Improbable Survivals', *Traditional Homes*, October, 136-140.

Roberts, S. (1977), 'Dovecotes in the Grand Manner', *Country Life*, 10 Feb, 322-323.

Rodgers, Frank (1956), 'Derbyshire Dovecotes', *Derbyshire Countryside*, 21, 4, 16-17.
    (1958), 'Staffordshire Dovecotes', *Staffordshire Life & County Pictorial*, Summer, 34.
    (1966), 'Our Fascinating Dovecotes', *Jnl. Mastic Asphalt Advisory Council*, 24-26.

Sapcote, Elwin S. (1946), 'Warwickshire Dovecotes', *Trans. Birmingham Archaeolog. Soc.*, 66, 122-126.

Saunders, Peter (1977), 'Dovecots', *Wiltshire Folklife*, 1, 2, 36-39.

Severn, J.A. (1987), 'Farm-based Tourism and Redundant Farm Buildings', *Jnl. of Historic Farm Buildings Group*, 1, 25-30.

Sheldrick, A.W. (1970), 'Dovecotes of Hertfordshire and the Saltpetre Industry', *Herts. Countryside*, May, 28.

Smith, Donald (1929), 'Essex Dovecotes', *The Essex Review*, 38, 180-183.
    (1932), 41, 178-181.
    (1933), 42, 132-135.
    (1934), 43, 97-100 & 152-155.
    (1935), 44, 229-232.
    (1941), 50, 103-105.

Smyth, Mary (1978), 'Tamar Dovecotes in 'Tamar'', *Jnl. of Friends of Morwellham*, 1, 14-19.

Spurr, H.R. (1959), 'Dove Houses as Social Monuments', *Derbyshire Countryside*, 24, 6, 14-15.

Suffield-Jones, N. (1966), 'Dovecotes and Gunpowder', *Surrey Archaeolog. Collections*, 63, 175.

Taylor, R.F. (1968), 'A Cob Dovecote at Durleigh', *Somerset Archaeolog. & Nat. Hist. Soc.*, 63, 101.

Thompson, W.A. (1982/3), 'Pimp Hall Dovecote, Chingford', *Essex Journal*, 17, 12-21.

'Tompkins Diary, The' (1930), *Sussex Archaeolog. Collections*, 71, 15-17.

Watkins, A. (1890), 'Herefordshire Pigeon Houses', *Trans. Woolhope Naturalists' Field Club*, 9-23.
    (1891), 'Pigeon Houses in Herefordshire & Gower, *Archaeological Journal*, 48, 29-41.
    (1893), 'Ancient Dovecotes', *Trans. & Proc. of Birmingham Archaeology Soc.*, 19, 8-21.

Webb, Rev. John (1845), 'Notes on a Preceptory at Garway', *Archaeologia*, 31, 182.

Westerling, Margaret (1939), 'Dovecotes in Gloucestershire', *Gloucestershire Countryside*, 3, 506-508.

Whitelaw, Jeffrey W. (1968), Dovecotes of Hertfordshire', *Hertfordshire Countryside*, 23, Oct, 26-28.
    (1969), 'Northamptonshire Dovecotes', *Northants Life*, Apr/May, 16-19.
    (1968/9), Dovecotes of East Anglia, *East Anglian Magazine*, 28, 398-402.

Whitnall, F.G. (1968), 'An Essex 'Duffus'', *Essex Countryside*, 16, Feb, 29.

Wittering, W.O. (1974), 'Dovecotes and Pigeon Lofts of Hertfordshire', *Hertfordshire Countryside*, 14, Jan, 40.

Yates, E. (1943), 'Manorial Pigeon Houses', *South Eastern Naturalist & Antiquary*, 48, 15-19.

Zestorsky, P.I. (1949), 'Esquisses d'Architecture Afghane', *Afghanistan*, 4, 3, 22 et seq.

# Ephemera

Abel-Smith, Julia (1987), 'Pavilions in Peril', *SAVE Britain's Heritage*.

Almond, T.L. (1986), Buchanan Prize Essay on 'Dovecotes', Assoc. of Northumberland Local History Societies, Morpeth.

Avoncroft Museum of Buildings (1984), Frontispiece of Newsletter, February, shows dovecote from Haselour Hall restored at Museum.

Bevington, J.D. (1983), 'Shropshire Dovecotes', The Caradoc & Severn Valley Field Club — Discovery Folder No. 2.

Broughton Dovecote, Hampshire. Excellent illustrated and descriptive pamphlet, available locally.

Collins, Phyllis (1972). 'Dovecotes with particular reference to the dovecotes of Northamptonshire.' A thesis for the City of Leicester College of Education, held by the Record Office, Delapré Abbey, Northampton.

*Cumberland News* for 23 July 1932. 'The Dovecots of Cumberland.'

Dunster Dovecote, Somerset. Illustrated pamphlet, available locally.

Frain, Susan (1985), 'The Pigeon Tower', *West Pennine Moors Newsletter*, June, Issue 4, p.3.

*Georgian Arcadia (Architecture for the Park and Garden)* (1987), Catalogue of an exhibition to mark the Golden Jubilee of the Georgian Group; several dovecotes included.

Godber, Joyce, *Willington Dovecote and Stable: Tudor Farm Buildings*, National Trust publication.

*Hangleton Manor Dovecote: History and Restoration* (1988), Hangleton Manor Dovecote Restoration Committee, Hove Borough Council.

Harrison, Reginald (1973), 'The Dovecote', an unpublished manuscript held by the Ancient Monuments Society, St Andrews-by-the-Wardrobe, London; about 18,000 words; 33 monochrome photographs; 60 scraperboard sketches.

Hunter, Mansel H. (1927), 'Neath and District Antiques — Dovecotes', *Swansea & Glamorgan Herald and Herald of Wales*, 19 and 26 November.

Maddock A.J., 'Pigeons for Food', one of a series of 32 Guide Cards to accompany the Norfolk Heritage booklet, *Food from the Land*.

Shropshire Libraries, Local Studies Department, Shrewsbury. Collection of dovecote photographs taken by local photographic society, circa 1947.

Thorndyke, Michael A. (1983), 'Poultryman's Kingdom', Letter in *Country Life*, 25 August, about Cilwendeg Farm pigeon house.

Waterton, Charles, 'Dovecotes in Yorkshire', manuscript from the L.M. Wilde Collection (1950) at RCHM, Fortress House, London.

Watkins, A. & Morgan, F., a collection of dovecote photographs held by Hereford City Library.

Whitworth, A. (1986), *A Concise Bibliography of Dovecotes and Pigeon Lofts*, a six-page illustrated booklet, privately published by British Dovecote Society, Weymouth.

Wilde, L.M. (1950), unpublished collection of illustrations and notes on dovecotes in three volumes, held by the RCHM, London.

# Index

Page numbers are given in medium type, black-and-white plate numbers in italic and colour plate numbers in bold.